Betty's Battle

Betty's Battle

A TRUE STORY OF DEPRESSION AND SCHIZOPHRENIA

B. S. Ruoss

To order additional copies of this book, contact:
Xlibris
1-888-795-4274
www.Xlibris.com
Orders@Xlibris.com
780719

Advance Acclaim
for Betty's Battle

"Betty's Battle, is truly a testimony of ones struggles and victory over mental health issues. This book will encourage those who face day-to-day mental health challenges to never give up on themselves nor the doctor that's treating them."

---Daisy Briggs Aldridge, MA, LLP, Owner
Daisies 4 U Adult Day Center

"Betty's book is an example of the ability to persevere and be able to come out on the other side with great insight and gratitude. Betty is so transparent in her own failures and lessons learned that one is inspired to know they can get to a better place in their own lives. Although anyone with mental health issues will benefit from reading this book, I believe all can learn from the many lessons learned and the understanding that we all need the help from others to make it in this life."

---Carol Gration/RN/CSM
Easterseals Michigan

"It gives me great pleasure to heartily endorse *Betty's Battle* by Betty Ruoss. Her story is a powerful one, and her account shows her tremendous strength and courage in persevering through significant challenges. Betty describes her early experiences in confronting racial and gender issues, and her perspective illustrates changes in treatment of the mentally Ill. It is particularly fascinating to see her perception of what was happening with her in contrast to what was recorded by the mental health professionals who she encountered. This is an important work that will be of great interest to the general public, as well as students and professionals in mental health who should read this to understand the effects of their words and actions on consumers with mental illness. And of course this book offers hope and encouragement to other consumers. Thank you"

---Laura D. Hirshbein, MD, PhD, Professor, Adult Psychiatry
Impatient Unit (9C) Medical Director
University of Michigan Department of Psychiatry

"Betty, your story powerfully portrays what an individual is personally experiencing with mental illness and its symptoms. Your story also shows your determination not to give up and keep working on and moving forward in your recovery. It gives others hope. Thank you Betty for sharing your experiences and life story with us."

---Vicki Suder, Director of Rights & Advocacy
Oakland Community Health Network

"This is Betty's personal account of the struggles, setbacks, and battles in the war to accept and manage her mental illness. Read about her overcoming the fears and stigma of this chronic illness."

---Sharynn Meltzer, LMSW/Case Manager
Easterseals Michigan

Contents

A Note to the Reader

The reader will find in the Glossary of Terms, pages 95-104, certain words defined as they are used in the text.

Acknowledgements

Schizophrenia can keep you in a "world of your own." However, I am blessed to know that God has always been with me and blessed to have family and friends who were not physically with me through my illness, but who wanted to and could have been if not for me.

Thanks to the many hospitals for supplying me with supporting records to include in my book.

Special thanks to Deloris and Alfred who never forgot me since the beginning of our friendship. She would have been there, when I really needed someone, if only she had known.

My brother and sister who wanted to be there but I didn't communicate with them.

A special thanks to Oakland Community Health Network for making it possible for me to have Mental Health Services.

Thanks to all the professional people who are in my life to offer support and services. Thank you Easterseals Michigan case managers, psychiatrists, and therapists, Easterseals Dreams Unlimited Clubhouse, group home providers, social workers and caregivers.

Thank you Katy, from Easterseals, for coming up with the title for this book.

Thank you Michael, who always wanted to be there, for bringing hope, encouragement and love into my life at the right time.

And thank you Irene, from Easterseals Dreams Unlimited Clubhouse, for taking time out of your busy schedule to edit this book for me. Also, thank you Estelle Green, from Easterseals Michigan, for your editing help, and thank you Michael for your help in editing this book.

I thank Mrs. Camilla and all those who provided me with encouragement while writing this book.

Foreword

I'll like to share my story of what I experienced as a person with depression and paranoid schizophrenia and to prove to you that one who has these illnesses can live a normal life with the right psychotropic meds and therapy.

I fell into schizophrenia when I was twenty-eight. I always had mild symptoms of a mental illness in my early years but not like what I experienced later in life. I was chronically depressed most of my adult life. Doctors never diagnosed me as depressive until thirty-four years later. My illness destroyed my marriage. It also caused me to lose jobs and friends.

My schizophrenia has included hallucinations, delusions, OCD, anxiety, co-dependency, weight change, sleep changes, mania (spending too much/heightened energy), strange behavior, no motivation, self-esteem problems, and isolation, added to depression.

As of this writing, I am sixty seven years of age. And, as long as I can remember, I have suffered from mental illness. The hardest battle has been most of my adult life.

I have been on several different kinds of medications - Seroquel, Celexa, Geodon, Depakene, Haldol, Valium, Abilify, Thorazine, Stelazine, Olanzapine and Zyprexa. I have been hospitalized seven times; two two-week stays, two one month stays, and the longest stay was for five consecutive years - 1995 to 2000 - in three different hospitals. Back then you were kept in psychiatric hospitals longer and didn't get the opportunity to get out. It wasn't until a 2010 hospitalization when I was prescribed a combination of Venlafaxine, Risperdal and Trazodone which helped me tremendously with my psychosis.

There are a number of events in my life which caused my condition to flare up, such as upbringing, stress from many things (including blindness), financial problems, joblessness and loneliness. I was homeless three times. I have encountered mistreatment by the police, whereas, I lost sight in one eye because of this. I had an arrest record and have been through a lot. I've had a hard life but the Lord was on my side and the Lord knows how much one can bear. He won't put on you any more than you can bear. I am a strong believer in our Lord.

Regardless of this illness, I have received many awards and have achieved many accomplishments in life. I was a civil rights activist in the 1960's. I have a BA Degree in Business Management & Economics from Shaw University. I attended Clark College, Atlanta University and have worked on my Master's Degree at Siena Heights University. I attended many vocational schools where I completed courses and was awarded certificates. I have traveled half-way around the world three times and presently I am enjoying my golden years by keeping active, being on committees, working out at the gym, entering sweepstakes as a hobby and spending time with my significant other.

I hope this book will be helpful for those who struggle with schizophrenia or depression, for health care workers, social workers, therapists, psychiatrists, and all those who want to know how this illness can affect one and how treatment can help.

The real names of people in this book have been changed to protect their privacy and identity.

Part I

SOUTHERN GIRL

I was born in Laurens County Georgia. Laurens County is a rural area of Georgia considered as the "country." It is located between Dublin, Georgia and Macon, Georgia and is approximately 121 miles from Atlanta. When I was younger, Atlanta was known as "Little New York." However, Macon was the big city to the people living in Laurens County. This was the place to move to from the country. It was considered as the "city" to us.

My dad was an only child. He, my mother and my siblings and I lived with his mother and father in a three room shotgun house which had a living room, bedroom and kitchen. The toilet was outside and we had well water. Grandpa Jim was a sharecropper, so our home sat on Mr. Thorndale's farmland near a railroad track. Whenever I hear a train whistle blow today, it saddens me. I never wanted to live in the country, even as a child.

I wasn't born in a hospital. My mother had a midwife deliver me. The midwife's name was Betty, so my parents named me after her. I was a pretty healthy baby, except for the fact I grew up nearsighted most of my life, and I inherited schizophrenia. Schizophrenia was, possibly, inherited from both my parents. Dad experienced schizophrenia when I was, maybe, twelve. We had moved to a new house, and it must have been too stressful for my dad. He couldn't recognize that we had moved. I can remember him having schizophrenic symptoms. He lived as if he was in our same old house. He wasn't hospitalized, but he did see a doctor. The doctor prescribed some large red pills for him. He was out of touch with reality for years. My mother told us children that he was taking the pills for his nerves. Mom showed signs of paranoid schizophrenia all her life. She always complained about the neighbors, and how they were doing mean things to her behind her back to hurt her, and how they talked about her. The neighbors didn't appear to me and others to be this way. She never saw a doctor for her condition, because she believed she was normal. Schizophrenia runs in my family, but fortunately my sister has not suffered from the disease.

When I was very young, around three or four years old, mom and dad moved us to Macon. During my childhood my family lived in four rented homes before I reached the age of nineteen. All homes were in Macon. Two of the residences were housing projects. The school children made jokes about our moving so much. Saying, "we must not be paying our rent" or "we got kicked out."

I first experienced a feeling of abandonment at the age of four when Mom and Dad left me in Laurens County with my grandparents for a few days because they wanted to take a trip together, alone. My brother and sister had gone to their friends to stay. I knew that my parents would return and bring me back home, but I couldn't take being without them for a few days. I felt so "left alone."

When they left the house I watched them leave from my bed, but didn't want them to see my face. When I said goodbye, I pulled the covers over my head so they wouldn't see me cry. I was ashamed. I have always been somewhat independent all of my life but there is always a feeling I carry of having to have "someone to be with." My grandparents' house was always a joy to visit because Grandpa gave me all the candy I could eat. But this particular time I just couldn't stand to be left alone with them. The smallest moment can have an impact on a child's life; this must have left its scar.

I grew up very fast. In grade school, I worked for my first grade teacher, Mrs. Thompson, as a house cleaner on Saturdays. I worked for her until I reached twelfth grade. She was a fair teacher. Even though I worked for her I was treated like the other students in my classroom. I wasn't the "teacher's pet."

Mom and Dad raised us children on an average income. We were at about the medium level.....neither poor nor rich. I was not satisfied with just getting by. In order to have more than the basic necessitates that I got at home, I had to buy the extras myself. I wasn't making a lot of money being a child, but I did make just enough to buy myself hot lunches at school from the cafeteria and some of the "trendy clothes" like the other kids wore. I can remember being ashamed to go to school without a lunch. I very seldom got money from my parents for lunches but they did give me money for milk and school supplies. I either brought my lunch from home or ate in the cafeteria. I would buy a sweater or shoes like the other kids wore, using the stores' layaway plans. But, when Dad didn't have money to buy us clothes, I wore plenty of hand-me-downs from the lady Mom worked for.

I received pretty good grades in elementary school – except for second grade. I failed the second grade, but was top student in third grade and from then on in school. By second grade I had become extremely near-sighted, but did not know I couldn't see well, until my third grade teacher noticed my squinting and walking up to the blackboard to read it. She told my mother to have my eyes checked. Mom and Dad took me to an ophthalmologist and I was given glasses. They always made sure that we had medical attention when we needed it. From then on, I wore contact lenses or eye glasses. I was extremely nearsighted most of my life. I bought my first pair of contact lenses during my senior year of high school. During my school years the kids, not once, called me four-eyed. So I didn't suffer from that.

I was very ambitious, even as a child. I finished elementary school with many achievement certificates. I went to Vacation Bible School most summers, and once to a day camp where I got a swimming award. I always wanted to be a movie star and had dreams of living better than what I knew. My heart was set on leaving home someday for New York.

Word got around the school that I worked for my first grade teacher. By eighth grade, in addition to cleaning up on Saturdays for Mrs. Thompson, I also worked for Mrs. Kessler, my fifth grade teacher. I cleaned her house Saturday afternoons after leaving Mrs. Thompson's house. As you can see, I had a busy work schedule, in addition to going to school and having to keep up my grades. I kept this up until my senior year in high school.

My dad had to leave his job when I was in ninth grade, and we lived on his disability payments and Mom's house cleaning salary until he passed away. My dad had worked as a painter of airplane parts for the Air Force. When he worked he used Friday's paychecks after work to get drunk. He stayed drunk the whole weekend. He was an alcoholic. Mom had to meet him after work on Friday just so he wouldn't spend all his money on drinking before taking care of the house. He and Mom would often have fights over his paycheck. Mom once sent him to the Emergency Room. They had a fight and she stabbed him in the arm with a pair of scissors. I was watching.

All through school I took trips to visit my grandparents in Laurens County. Now I had the courage to spend summer vacations and take holiday trips to visit them regardless of my episode at age four. Even in elementary school, I was mature enough to take the Greyhound Bus alone from Macon to the country to visit them. Grandma and Grandpa always gave me spending money when I needed it, and they fed me all the food I could eat, and anything I wanted to eat, when I visited them. Grandpa was a help to my father in taking care of us until he died of heart failure in 1966. Dad also passed three months after my grandfather from cirrhosis of the liver. I didn't show any emotion at my dad's funeral, but I took my grandfather's death pretty hard. My therapist tells me today I had no emotional involvement with my dad. Therefore, I showed no emotion at his funeral.

I never learned to pray from my family. I did however, watch grandma pray, and watched Mom get down on her knees to pray. Nonetheless, I did attend Sunday school at an early age, and was baptized Baptist around the age of ten. I didn't develop a personal relationship with God until much later in life.

Mom taught me "yes ma'am" and "no ma'am", "thank you", "excuse me", and how to wash and wear clean clothes. Especially clean underwear in case "I got sick out", she said. I kept myself clean, did my own hair and wore clean clothes, and paid for things I needed even at an early age. I never got a "pat on the back" from Mom for anything I did. She always bragged on my schoolmates and children I knew, but never praised me for anything. She always "put me down." She would point out how my friends looked, but never said how pretty I looked. I tried to live up to her downplay. I have learned to forgive her for that. When I grew up, kids were treated a lot differently than today. There weren't a lot of hugs and kisses and praises from the parents. Mom never praised me when I got good grades in school, either. This stayed with me for a long time. I had no strong family support. The first time and only time I celebrated my birthday was around seven years old. One of Mom's employers sent me a cake for my birthday. One of my closest friends was over. I slipped and fell off the stool I was sitting on and dropped my slice of cake on the floor. All my mother did was stand there laughing hysterically at me. I was so ashamed, I cried. I never forgot that moment.

All throughout life I have had reasons to believe that my mother just didn't care about me. She treated my brother and sister much better. I am the last born child and I believe that, when I came into this world, all the joy that children bring to mothers had just worn off of her.

I got very few beatings, but when I did do something wrong, Mom whipped me with a wet towel or pinched me until it hurt. I was very young when this happened and I still have memories of it. Once I was playing around in the bath tub as she bathed me, and she wanted me to stop moving around. She whipped me with the wet towel. Another time I didn't want her to comb my hair, so she cut off my locks. She knew that I loved my long sandy hair. Most times, I was a good and obedient child. I now recognize I was a victim of child abuse. I can't really blame her for her actions, and how she brought me up because, more than likely, she may have been brought up in the same manner herself. Dad gave me a lashing with his belt once when he was alive. He did this because I didn't wash the dishes when he asked me to. For some unknown reason, I wanted him to whip me, because he never once had to. Even though Dad drank a lot, he was the favorite of my parents. I don't hold neither Mom nor Dad's parenting against them now. I have forgiven them.

My imagination was unusual for a child in the first grade. The class had to rest every day at school. Not quite asleep with my head on my desk, many times I vividly imagined a man being tortured hanging on a cross about to be castrated. This thought came only in school during rest time. I never understood why I thought this way, until my therapist recently explained why this happened. She says "I thought this way because this was something I had heard from older people and that I had picked up negative energy going around from them. Black men were treated badly back then….with disrespect. So I was visualizing what I had heard from people." At a young age, I also saw all kinds of animals in my room at night as I was semi-asleep. It seemed very real. Each piece of furniture in my room was an animal. I still remember it. My therapist said "to release it."

By the age of thirteen, I was drinking liquor and smoking cigarettes. My brother, Hargrove, was an accomplished guitar player. He was in a local rock band playing in night clubs around Macon and nearby towns. I, along with my two girlfriends, would go to gigs with him on weekends and some week nights. During the week nights we got home after 3:00 am. I never missed school the next day, though. But I did go to class hung over. We were underage to go to night clubs, but we got inside the clubs by saying we were with the band. By doing this, the owner couldn't put us out. Plus, during my time, children grew up fast, although I never developed a real taste for liquor. I was never an alcoholic.

I had a voice for singing then, so once in a while I had the opportunity to sing with the band. I was told that this would be too rough a life for me to consider as a career. I regret today this advice influence my decision. Who knows, someday I might have been a famous singer. Even though I had fun at the clubs, I finished Junior High School with honors. I continued to go out with Hargrove and his band all through high school. I liked being around the older crowd. I was never interested in school boys or boys my age. My boy friends were usually servicemen or older than me.

I did know one boy in high school who wanted to be my boyfriend, and I did occasionally go out with him. Doug was a football player at school, but he wasn't old enough to be my boyfriend. So I left him for a military man. I always wanted an older man. Michael, my significant other today, changed this thinking. He is five years younger than me. I will discuss him later.

I was brought up on a short leash. I had strict morals. Meaning, "I didn't have sex with any of the guys I knew while in high school. Mom always told me to "keep my dress down" and don't have sex because "the boys would talk about you if you did or they would laugh at you if you got pregnant." I believed her. As a result, I was always a "good girl"…so to speak.

Throughout my high school years, I always had a need to have someone around me at school. If there wasn't a girlfriend there to talk to me, I felt alone and embarrassed. I was never part of a "clique." Every day before classes started, all the students would gather on what we called the "walkway", talking to one another. If I had no one to keep me company, I was uneasy. I had difficulty being part of a group. And I didn't make friends easily. I felt the same eating alone in the cafeteria. If Lorraine of Delphine, my closest two friends, were not at school, or had other friends they wanted to talk to instead of me that day, I didn't know what to do without them. It wasn't until I met Samuel that I felt part of a group. He had already finished high school, so he had the time to drive me to school. He would stand on the walkway with me, to keep me company until class started.

I met Samuel through one of my closest friends, Delphine. She was a member of the NAACP, and so was he. I met him at her house one summer evening. I was surprised to see that he was Caucasian. More so, being a guest at a Negro's house in the 60's in Georgia.

In addition to being a member of the NAACP he was also a member of the SCLC. He, along with other activists, was in Georgia to fight for Civil Rights. We hit it off right away. He was just what I had always wanted and he was six years older than me. It was love at first sight, or at least I thought I was in love. I joined the NAACP and became an activist in the civil rights movement.

I took part in meetings, boycotting establishments, sit-ins and marches along with him and others. We became good friends which was hard to do in the Deep South. We had to sneak around to be together. It was hard, but we had our own private places where we could be together. I had my share of pressure and fears from this relationship. It wasn't easy for my parents to accept, so that didn't make it any easier on me.

The KKK was aware of our friendship. We would often go to restaurants with other civil rights activists, and leave to find our car tires had been slashed. They also made threatening calls to my home, telling me what they were going to do to us. They called me names like Blackie and the 'N' word. They even threatened to bomb my house. By the grace of God no harm came to me. From then on, I kept watch "over my shoulder" as long as I lived in Georgia.

Samuel and I were close. He taught me many things I didn't know. He tried to take me to my Senior Prom but couldn't because he was told he was "never a student at my all Black high school." The principal felt it would cause problems for the school because he was White. We were quite disappointed.

I could have left the state, but I didn't want to leave Georgia yet. New York was always the place I wanted to be. Nonetheless, I stayed and finished high school in Georgia and continued to fight for civil rights. By my twelfth year in school, I was a straight-A student. I had earned enough credits to justify me spending only a half day in school….so I went to high school in the mornings only. I went to Vocational School at night and earned a certificate in Business/Shorthand. I finished top in my class. After completing this school, I spent the afternoons after school until evening, working in a job I got through the Job Corps. I was assigned to work as a secretary for the State. Now I had a real job, so I left my jobs working for the teachers. I had also had jobs before, cleaning a beauty salon and working as a bus girl in a restaurant. I was "in the door" and "out the door" on these jobs because this was not what I wanted to do for life.

I wanted to work and save money. I was always afraid of not having, so I wanted to be secure. I wanted to live better than how I was raised.

After working for the city, I took and passed the Civil Service Examination, and begin working for the Air Force close to where I lived. I was the only clerk on the Base in a job like mine. I issued, approved and signed (my name) to military drivers' licenses for servicemen and civilians who needed a license to drive for the Air Force. The job paid very well and was fulfilling. I worked on this job for more than a year.

Part II

NEW YORK, NEW YORK AND
A TASTE OF AFRICA

Samuel eventually left Georgia and moved to New York. He loved me very much and wanted me there.

I came across an opportunity to apply for a camp counselor position near Albany, New York which I accepted. I had always thought of living in New York, so this was my chance. I packed my belongings and boarded a Greyhound bus to New York. I worked as a camp counselor in charge of dysfunctional inner city kids. I wasn't much for the outdoors…so I didn't last very long on this job. I didn't feel at ease. I just couldn't "adjust" and was experiencing culture shock.

I was pretty much a professional, and had never worked with children, anyway, so I only lasted two months on this job. I went back to Georgia, and enrolled at Clark College in Atlanta. I had saved enough money for one year of college and I had my own car. I didn't stay in the dorm. Instead, I stayed with my sister and her family. I felt pretty alone in college because I didn't have a close friend. I experienced the same feelings that I always had in high school. I quit college after completing close to a year, and then got a job working for a bank in downtown Atlanta. After working a short time, I decided I wanted to go back to New York because it was more modern and liberal than Georgia. Samuel and I were married. I never knew love and couldn't accept his love. I was always paranoid around him, and around his family and friends. I felt they were plotting and planning against me. This was a sign of schizophrenia. These symptoms were not as severe as in my later years. Samuel and I had arguments. Most of them were my fault. I must have made his life miserable. Once we saw a marriage counselor to help our marriage. I attended one session and didn't return for any future visits because, I thought Samuel and the counselor were having conversations about me without my knowledge. Samuel and I eventually separated which led to a divorce.

I moved to a boarding house outside of New York City. The boarding house was okay, but this was not how I wanted to live. Frankly, I wanted a place of my own. I eventually took a job as an administrative assistant (called secretary back then) with a Fortune 500 Company. When I got this job, I made up my mind to stay with this company until retirement. My plan was to move up the corporate ladder. The Women's Liberation Movement helped to influence my thinking. I moved out of the boarding house into an apartment of my own.

It wasn't more than a few months that I had lived in my own apartment before it was burglarized. For my own safety I didn't want to stay in it any longer. A friend girl I had met invited me to move with her, at his mother's house, which was more than 30 miles away from my job. In New York the wait list for an apartment can run up to a year. I didn't want to move back to Georgia. I accepted my friend's invitation. I moved in with people I had just met. Even though they were good Christian people, I stayed under stress. I started to become paranoid about them. I kept my job and commuted back and forth from New Jersey to New York for a year. Then I moved out of my friend's mother's house. I found an apartment and moved to Westchester County, New York.

All of my life I wanted to work, make good money, and move up on the job. I always wanted to do better. I didn't let anything of anyone get in my way. I just wanted to do my own thing. I worked very hard at this.

I met guys where I worked, and I saw one man causally after work for dinner. Nothing came out of this relationship.

I had never built a serious relationship with a man since my divorce. Then I met a man who appealed to me. Aaron and I dated for two years and we talked of marriage. However, due to circumstances we never married. I became pregnant. Mentally, I was not ready to have a baby. More so I was never a maternal person. I didn't know what to do. I panicked and I was scared. I didn't want to give up my work, and I didn't have time for a child. I decided not to have the baby and chose to have an abortion instead. I didn't have any regrets about the abortion until much later in life when I realized what I had done. I had aborted my baby and instead of having the baby I purchased two dogs to take the place of it.

I continued working for the same company and moved up through the ranks. I advanced to the third corporate level secretarial position, working for a vice-president before transferring to Michigan in 1976. (I will discuss this later in the book.)

I became even more ambitious. I had always worked hard on the job and I tried to better myself. It was like I was trying to prove something. The company I worked for had a tuition refund program. I took advantage of this program by furthering my education. I enrolled at Shaw University in Connecticut to obtain a Bachelor of Arts Degree. The school was about forty miles each way from my New York apartment. I drove to Connecticut after work three evenings a week for three years attending night classes until I graduated with a BA in Business Management and Economics. I also drove to New York City every Friday evening, after work, for one year, all while attending college, to take acting classes. I earned a certificate in Acting.

I had always had a desire to travel. On my job I had accumulated quite a bit of vacation time, so I decided to take a trip. I went to East

Africa. I booked the trip for one on a guided safari to Kenya and Tanzania. There were other people, whom I didn't know from other parts of the United States who were also booked on the same safari. I met two girls my age -- one, who was from Maryland, and the other from Washington, D.C. The other people were older retirees on a vacation. A month before leaving on the trip I started to feel strange. I had never felt this way before. I became extremely frightened. I had a feeling that someone would harm me while in Kenya with voodoo. I became delusional. It got so bad that I couldn't stand to look at African movies or read anything on Africa without fear.

Nor was I able to look at the photo of a gentleman (Masanda), who had since moved back to Kenya, whom I had met years before in Detroit by a girlfriend on a visit. To me, his picture carried messages and was more than just a picture to look at. There was something "magical" about it, I felt. His picture scared me. It was just a picture of a man, but I couldn't stand to look at it. I was afraid to be alone in my apartment, and I was afraid to go to sleep. I wanted to cancel my trip but I had already paid for it, and couldn't back out without losing part of my money. So I ignored my feelings and went on the trip. It was a help to me to meet two girls on the trip.

Before flying into Nairobi we spent two nights in Brussels, Belgium. Barbara, Anna and I were together throughout the whole trip. I even saw Masanda for a few hours on a stop during the safari. Seeing him didn't upset me as much as I had anticipated. After the trip, Barbara, Anna and I exchanged addresses, so that we could travel together again. They contacted me a few times, but I didn't want to be bothered. I never returned their calls and I never saw them again.

Part III

A MOVE TO MICHIGAN AND
A DOWNWARD SPIRAL

In 1976, I was offered a promotion at a Branch Office in Detroit in marketing. I took the job and the company relocated me to Michigan. I had advanced from a Corporate senior secretarial job to the Marketing Division with the company. I gave up wanting to be an actress or singer. I left Aaron behind, and never saw him again.

As soon as I arrived in Michigan, I was put in an intense training program. I had to be trained for my new job in Marketing because it was so different from the secretarial position I left. In this new job, I had to teach the word processing equipment to the company's customers, give seminars to customers, make analyses and support the equipment as well as support sales representatives throughout my territory.

At the time I was in training, the company only gave me one month to find housing. Finding a place to stay was an effort, since I had brought my two big Samoyeds from New York with me. Dogs living in an apartment are very common in New York, but not in Michigan. I nearly ran out of time trying to find us a place to live

in. Near the end of my thirty-one days, a co-worker offered to rent
me a flat. I rented it from her. It had two floors. An accountant,
lived downstairs, and I lived on the upper floor. We had separate
entrances. As a result, the dogs weren't much of a bother to him. I
lived in this flat for a year. I moved because I determined my rental
payments were enough to go toward a mortgage. I was pretty upset.

I continued to go through training programs on-site for new
equipment the company invented. I also traveled to other states for
additional training, all while taking care of my other responsibilities.
I wasn't getting proper rest and I was burned out from the load. This
is when I fell into a real case of schizophrenia.

I stayed stressed out and my behavior was peculiar. I didn't have
a hygiene problem, but, I began to feel uncomfortable around people
especially when they got close to me. I would withdraw. I felt as if
I wasn't clean and had an odor even though I had bathed and was
wearing clean clothes. When I walked, I moved with so much speed
I had to be told to slow down. This wasn't normal at all. I felt uneasy
around everyone. I couldn't stand to be around people. I went to
lunch alone just to avoid my co-workers.

I didn't talk very much. I thought my co-workers were whispering
about me behind my back. I started to show stress in my face. My
manager noticed a difference in me. He asked me to take a day off
from work to take a break. He said, "You look like you are tired." He
was exactly right. I took the day off and I also took a vacation after
a break in my training. I went on another trip to Kenya.

This time I went alone, and I went to visit Masanda whom I had
met in the past. We had only known each other a short time before
he moved back to Kenya. There was love on his part, because shortly
after meeting him, he asked me to marry him. I never developed love
for him. I could think of no other place to go so I went to visit him.
I had gotten over the fears I had of him.

On my way to Kenya, I made two stopovers. My first stop was
in London. I had the time to sightsee. I took a sightseeing bus tour
alone and saw many of the tourist attractions. Later, I was on a plane
to Amsterdam, Holland. I walked around the city, took a canal tour,

saw the homes bordering the canals and other sites. Then I took a flight to Kenya the next morning.

When I arrived in Nairobi, Masanda was there waiting for me with open arms. We stayed in Nairobi the night before we left for his village in Voi, Kenya. It was just as you would expect Kenya to be…… mostly "bush," (that's what they call it) except for Nairobi. Masanda was considered a millionaire in his country. He had his own car, and he had built a three-room block brick house for us to live in. He had electricity, a telephone, indoor water pipes installed and a bathroom with a shower. Masanda also had propane stove for me to cook on, as well as a small refrigerator and a radio component set for listening to music.

Masanda tried to make it as "Americanized" as possible for me so I would stay there. We would have been considered the most modern couple living in Voi. Even with this, it was not like living in America, and it wasn't enough to make me stay. I missed the United States' foods, going shopping, and being in my own apartment. I missed everything.

I stayed in Kenya for three weeks. Kenya is alright to visit, but could never be my home. I took a flight back to the U.S. with stopovers. On the trip home, I had a stopover in Athens, Greece and Copenhagen, Denmark. I entertained myself with taking a bus to the City Centre. I walked the streets, going into the shops; buying clothes and souvenirs. When I was done, I took a city bus back to the airport and boarded the plane to the United States. I was never much of a social person. When I didn't have someone to be with me, I did most things alone. I was a very brave, daring, and independent individual. When I travelled, I felt free and alive.

Upon returning back to work the pressure of the job wasn't any less. I was always learning newly invented equipment, teaching classes, giving seminars, doing word processing studies, all along with managing a territory which was spread out as far as 60 miles from the office. It was often very late when I got home from work. The job was very stressful. When I got home I had to walk the dogs, and prepare dinner for myself. Then I went to bed, waking up the next morning with the same routine. I had very little time for a social life.

Plus, I had not met anyone outside of work. In my mind, I believed working as hard as I did would get me further ahead. I was like a wizard doing my job.

As I drove home from work one day I began to hear voices. It wasn't just one voice talking -- it was many -- in a low tone. I couldn't distinguish what they were saying to me. It sounded like a radio between stations, with a lot of static. I continued to hear voices in my head until they became clearer.

I had become more knowledgeable of the area now, so I moved out of the flat. I bought a condominium thirty miles north of Detroit in a very close-knit, quiet neighborhood. The residents consisted of mainly retirees, except for two families around my age. I later learned that I was the only single, female living there. This meant that I didn't have much in common with the neighbors.

I had no one to listen to me, nor talk to. I felt very alone and was depressed most of the time. I didn't want to go outdoors. This is when I started isolating myself. I had the same routine. I had to take my dogs out in the morning before work; again in the evening; TV; dinner; and back to work the next morning. This went on for the seven years I lived there. I didn't have but one boyfriend which lasted about two years while living there. He was the only person to visit me there, except for my family who rarely visited me from out of state. He visited with me every Sunday and had dinner with me at my house. I began to wonder if he was dating someone else. We were not really attracted to each other.

The only other outlet I had was work. I was so tense and bothered with voices in my head, that, in 1978, I realized I needed to see a psychiatrist. I started to feel like the people (especially managers) on the job were judging me to see how well I did my job so as to promote me. When I had to converse with the people at work, they had other intentions. I thought they were testing me. I felt they could read what I was thinking and that I could talk to them without opening my mouth.

One particular voice started to speak to me. I could hear it loud and clear in my head. The voice that I heard then, and mostly

throughout my illness, sounded like a child. It sounded like Alvin –
of "Alvin and the Chipmunks." I started to see Dr. Charleston, a
psychiatrist. I telephoned my family often, who lived out of state, but
I never mentioned to them what I was going through because I knew
they couldn't help me. I saw Dr. Charleston for psychotherapy sessions
once a week. I was treated with different psychotropic medications.
He started me on Valium to calm me first, but this didn't work. Even
with meds, I continued to exhibit strange behavior, especially on the
job. He gave me the Minnesota Phase Personality Test and other
therapies.

The test results showed I was a person with paranoid
schizophrenia. At least, that was his diagnosis. He also told me that
I could become stressed out over anything. He discontinued the
Valium and prescribed a high dosage of Thorazine. Thorazine is an
antipsychotic medication. It didn't stop me from hearing voices. Plus,
I didn't continue taking the medication because I had a reaction from
it. Thorazine kept me sleepy, hindering me from working a full day.
It also kept my nose plugged. Dr. Charleston changed my medication
to Stelazine, another antipsychotic medication. I couldn't take this,
either.

At the time I was taking Stelazine, I was experiencing thought
disorders. My mind was racing. I was thinking extremely fast, racing
from one thought to another; making irrational statements. My
thoughts were disorganized and didn't make sense. My head felt
hollow. I was teaching a class once, and my words were scattered and
not structured. I was saying things that didn't make sense in front
of the students. I had to excuse myself from the class and go home.
Stelazine didn't help me at all. That's when Dr. Charleston admitted
me to St Mary's Hospital Psychiatric ward in August, 1978. This was
my first hospitalization. I was hospitalized for two weeks.

After my discharge, I returned to work still stressed and anxious.
Dr. Charleston prescribed a lower dosage of Thorazine this time.
Thorazine still didn't help me. I continued to experience symptoms of
schizophrenia. For instance, when I saw my primary physician, (not
for psychotropic meds though), or had to wait in a waiting room, I

thought I was being watched. As I sat in the waiting room to be called, I thought cameras were installed in the walls, to see how I would act. I still heard voices. This continued for years. Nonetheless, I took the Thorazine when I wanted to, and continued to see Dr. Charleston until he retired and closed his practice six years later. Back then, there weren't a whole lot of psychotropic medicines available.

My illness didn't stop me from traveling though. In December of 1978, I took my third trip to Africa. Again I went to Voi, Kenya to visit Masanda. On my way there I stopped in London, England again, and saw pretty much the same things. From England I went to Paris, France, took a train into the city and stayed for a while. I walked around the town as if I was one of the locals. From Paris I flew to Geneva, Switzerland. I took a taxi from the airport to the hotel, where I stayed in a hotel in the international meeting section of town. Geneva is so small, I was able to walk around the town sightseeing. Since it was around Christmas, the town was all lit up and decorated with Christmas lights. I had planned to be in Nairobi by Christmas and I arrived there a day before.

Masanda wasn't expecting me to arrive when I did, so he wasn't there to meet me at the airport. I went to the 680 Hotel in Nairobi, which I knew so well, and stayed for the night. I wanted to surprise Masanda, so I took a hired car to his village the next morning. I made it there, over 300 miles from Nairobi. This time I stayed in Kenya for four weeks. When I left, Masanda didn't want me to return back to the U.S. again, but I did. I wasn't in love enough with him to give up my life in the United States. When I returned home, we corresponded by mail and telephone for five years. Then I got a letter from him saying he was "married and his first born was on the way." I didn't respond, so that's the last time I heard from him.

I continued to work for the same company until I was fired in 1980. I really don't think I deserved to be fired because I had been an outstanding employee since the day I was hired. Since, I started my job in marketing support, I had gotten many awards and salary raises. I had three different marketing managers since being there. My last manager left the state. Therefore, I was under a new manager.

Edwin came into the department from a Central US branch office. He was in a different position there. Now he was my manager. He gave me a substantial workload as soon as he came on the job. Most of the tasks assigned to me involved having to write out how to do my job. This went on for months. Nonetheless, I always did my work correctly and met all deadlines required of me. In the beginning, I thought he was grooming me for a promotion, because my goal was to become a manager someday. I thought that maybe I was a threat to him. I began to believe that I was being forced to resign….but I didn't resign.

The day I was fired, I had to turn in my keys to the building, my ID, demonstration books and the keys to my file cabinet. I can't even remember Edwin telling me that I was fired. I assumed that I was fired when I had to return my business items to him. The company had invested quite a bit of money in me for something like this to have happened. I found myself becoming more stressed, exhausted, delusional, and I continued to hear voices. The loss of my job was a traumatic experience. I still have nightmares of it today. I will always believe Edwin used my knowledge to do his job or passed it on to a lady who had transferred in from overseas who had nothing to do until I left. As I drove home that day, I was hearing voices. A voice told me to drive into the brick wall (median) separating the lanes on the expressway to have an accident. I couldn't bring myself to do this. But I came pretty close.

I went back to Dr. Charleston and told him what had happened. I was instructed to tell Edwin that I was seeing a psychiatrist, and that I was sick so that I could at least get my job back. When I went there I was instructed to talk to the medical assistant for the Branch Office. Mr. Green telephoned the company psychiatrist in Chicago. Being that I was not in Chicago, the psychiatrist couldn't treat me, my situation was dropped. I left and never went back to the company again.

In my condo, the neighbors watched everything that went on there. At least, that's what I thought. I didn't want my neighbors to find out that I didn't have a job to go to. Luckily for me, I had attended night classes in 1979 after working during the day, and obtained my license as a real estate sales person. Now I was out of a job so this license came in handy. I combed the wanted ads of the Detroit News to find a job. Maxwell & Associates, a Commercial and Industrial Real Estate Company had an ad under "Sales Jobs." I applied for a Commercial/Industrial Sales Person position with the company, and was hired. I really wasn't up to working. I was still stressed and tired from my previous job. I was hearing voices and still acting paranoid, but I made myself get up every morning and drive to work. I felt that my neighbors would know I had a job if I did this. I thought they had been keeping track of me, because all the time I lived there, they watched me going to work every day.... or so I thought.

I started to suffer from OCD. When I had to leave the house, I checked my lock several times before leaving to see if it was working properly and locked securely. When I got half way to where I was going, I would turn around and go back home to check the lock again. I constantly checked my lock when I was home as well. Dr. Charleston kept me on the Thorazine meds to block out these symptoms but it didn't help. Like before, I had so many side effects from this medication, I just stopped taking it on my own, and I didn't tell him. My condition got worse. I was listening to voices all the time while still trying to carry on everyday life, but I didn't think I was sick.

In real estate you are not paid until a sale is made – and I was accustomed to receiving a pay check. Therefore, I got a job at Michigan Business Institute teaching business courses to bring in a steady paycheck. I could set my own hours in the real estate job, being an independent contractor, so I worked in real estate from mid-afternoon until the evening and taught school from morning until noon.

I had not worked more than a month at the school when one day the voice told me to "stay home." I just couldn't bring myself to go to work that day. I called the principal, Mrs. Eaton, saying "I had personal things to take care of" in a not so pleasant tone. I was angry with her for no reason. What I really wanted to do was to isolate myself inside the house. I was out two days. On the day I returned to work, Mrs. Eaton was teaching my class. She had not been able to hire a substitute teacher on such a short notice. Mrs. Eaton was not pleased because I was out and because she had to teach the class. She fired me.

I continued working at the real estate company in an area of real estate I had to learn. Mr. Maxwell was very considerate and very patient in working with me. I wasn't the easiest person to be around at that time. My biggest faults were "not listening, and doing things my way," he told me. This was because I listened to voice(s). I had problems when dealing with my clients. I felt I had some special power. I felt that I could read their minds, and they could read my mind. So I was cautious about my thinking.

When I read a book, or looked at anything in writing, certain words would stand out and look highlighted on the page. I felt this was a message being shown to me. I kept this to myself. Mr. Maxwell never knew how I felt and what I was experiencing. I sold a few properties, but didn't make enough money to live on. I had a pretty big savings account and stocks and bonds to back me up, though. Money wasn't the issue in the beginning. I kept spending money as if I was still receiving a pay check. I thought my life would get better. But it did not.

My social life didn't get any better – work, home, walking Samantha and Sham then to bed in isolation. Actually my life had become worse.

I never accepted the fact that I had a mental illness, so I continued to try to work. I applied for a teacher's position at McCullum Business College and was hired. Again, I taught business courses and worked from morning until afternoon, then after classes at the real estate company. The voices got worse. I was so stressed out and tired from hearing them and from reacting to what I heard.

They told me things about other people and what they were doing to me. I heard voices of many people. Then, sometimes, I heard just one voice telling me what to do. This got very bad; I wasn't able to keep up with grading my students' papers. I had also become very argumentative. Once, I punished a student unnecessarily because she was late for my class. Sue had a good reason for being late, but I didn't believe her. She complained to the principal about me. He took her side. I was afraid that I would get fired eventually, so I resigned before this happened. I lied to Mr. Stewart, the principal, saying "I was moving out of town."

I continued to see Dr. Charleston. He knew everything going on in my life. But I never told him I was not taking the medicine he prescribed and how bad the voices had gotten. I didn't throw the prescriptions he wrote for me away. I kept them in a drawer in my bedroom. I was seeing him once every two months now because I didn't have any insurance.

I felt like I could communicate with people without talking and that I could read their minds, and they could tell what I was thinking, too. With this and obsessed with hearing voices, I started to feel I was possessed by an "evil spirit" and that the devil needed to come out of me. I felt I needed an exorcism. I looked in a spiritual newspaper and found the name of an exorcist. I asked him if he would perform an exorcism on me. Mr. Parrish said he "wasn't sure if he could make the evil spirit come out of me, but he surely would try." We set a date for me to see him. Right before the appointment date, I started to get scared. I was worried that something might go wrong in the exorcism, so I didn't see him. Nor did I call to let him know I wasn't coming. I thought I could handle this myself. I prayed to seek the Lord. I became very spiritual, believing prayer kills anything evil. I listened to religious radio stations and watched religious TV shows.

I stayed anxious. The voice(s) kept me running like a "wild person", trying to do what I heard. I tried meditation class, but this didn't help. I only got worse. I began to worry about what the future had in store for me. I knew that people went to fortune tellers to see what the future holds for them. As a matter of fact, two ladies at the Fortune 500 Company had seen one on their lunch break when I worked there. They gave me her name. I saw Lillie, and had my future read. As of today, I am still waiting for her predictions to happen.

Then I looked in the yellow pages, and found an astrologist in Royal Oak. I made an appointment with her and kept it. Rebecca gave me a reading looking through a crystal ball, a card reading, handwriting, and a tea leaf reading. She charged me $125.00, because she spent a while with me and typed up a report of my future. Rebecca was about eighty years old and ailing. When I picked up the report, it was very interesting. She told me about how the moon affects my astrological sign, and all. I had a hard time figuring it out. She gave very little information about my future, as I can remember as of this writing. But she did tell me, from reading her cards that "I would be sitting in a home having dinner with a group of women." This prediction turned out to be true, I thought, because I have lived in a group home with women, and our meals were together, sitting at a table. This may have been a coincidence. (I will talk about the group homes later in the book.) Nothing else, as I can remember, came true.

Rebecca was a very lonely lady. She lived alone. She befriended me and started calling me every now and then. I didn't try to see her again until 1985.

I had nearly run out of my savings. But I continued to go to Dr. Charleston until he retired that year (1984). He gave me a list of psychiatrists to choose from for me to continue therapy....but I never contacted any of them, not even one. As a matter of fact, I never saw a psychiatrist again until 1995. Until then I was never on any psychotropic medications – or any medications at all. I didn't think I needed any. In my world, I was healthy and normal.

I moved from my condo to Atlanta in the fall of 1984. I had flown Samantha and Sham, my two Samoyed dogs, to Georgia a year before me. I had gotten tired of them. Hargrove and Mom took care of them at their home for me. That took the pressure and load of having to take care of them off me because I started to feel someone would report me to the authorities. I thought they would say I wasn't taking good care of them, even though I was taking good care of them.

I no longer wanted to live in my condo, because I still felt the neighbors were watching every move I made. And I thought my next door neighbors were after me. I began to hear knocking sounds on my bedroom wall, which I thought was coming from them. This knocking noise was all in my mind.

I moved to Georgia to stay with Hargrove and Mom. I put my condo on the market with a real estate company. I sold all my furniture and put all my personal items in storage. I flew mom to Michigan earlier to accompany me to Georgia for company. I hooked up a trailer to my BMW and transported all my clothes and shoes down south. Mother couldn't drive, so I drove the whole trip. This took nearly fourteen hours. All the while I drove, I listened to the voices. I thought the cops were following me the whole trip. This was also in my mind.

We stopped at a hotel in Kentucky to spend the night. Not more than five hours had passed when I frantically woke mother up. I thought the people in the next room were listening to us and they wanted us out because we were Black. Mom said she "didn't hear anything." She didn't know I was hallucinating. I ran to the lobby desk and checked us out. Mom just got up and left with me. I had not gotten any sleep, but we made it to Atlanta safely, by the grace of God.

In Atlanta, I shared a room with mom. Since I had always lived alone after my divorce this was not exactly the lifestyle I wanted. I quickly found out. I had always wanted to better myself. In order to make use of my time while there I went to school. I enrolled in a Disc Jockey training course at Atlanta University. I completed the course, and received my certification and my FCC License. I also attended a Tax Preparation Course, and achieved the second highest grade in the class.

It seemed to me my mother didn't like the idea I was attending school. She criticized me for studying all hours of the night, and made comments like "are you still going to school?" Since she didn't have the opportunity to finish high school, she showed some jealousy towards me. She didn't respect my having to study to pass the courses.

My concentration and memory was not good because of my illness. Because of this I needed peace and quiet to do my homework, which she didn't allow. She turned the TV volume up loud or continuously talked to me while I studied, knowing I wanted her to stop. This was very irritating. She did this purposely, because she didn't want me to get more education.

Her jealousy didn't stop me though; I went on to get a Georgia Real Estate License. I completed a real estate course at a school of real estate, passed the State Exam and received my license.

Mom also showed her favoritism for my sister while I lived with her. For example, she knew that I was a coupon saver. She started to save coupons like me. When she had saved a few, she gave them to my sister, saying to me, "You don't need these, you've got enough." This made me feel really bad. This is when I started doubting that I was her child. The voices made me believe that I was adopted. In my head I started to believe this and I didn't stop when she died in 2006.

I believed all kinds of thoughts that were in my head. I even believed, in my mind, that I was the daughter of a Caucasian lady she had worked for and that my mom raised me for her. No one could tell me I wasn't Mrs. Mae's child. I didn't hate Mom, nor do I have a feeling of hatred for her now....I just didn't want to be near her any longer. I just wanted to get away from there, to be on my own again.

After I had been in Georgia a year, I heard from the realtors who listed my condo, saying that "they had an offer." I accepted the offer by telephone, but I had to go back to Michigan for the closing. Early one morning, I got in my car – not telling my family I was leaving, and headed for Michigan, alone. I left the dogs in Georgia. I drove the whole trip, only stopping for gas and once at a rest stop. As I drove, I was seeing things happening on the expressway that seemed real to me at the time. I thought I saw two men on the side of the expressway changing a tire on their car as soon as I left Atlanta. Later, I saw the same car and two men further up the road doing the same thing. Now I realize this couldn't have been, because I had left the men behind me, and I know they couldn't have passed me on the road that quick. I drove on I-75 until I got to Detroit. It took me thirteen hours to get to Michigan.

When I arrived in Southfield, I was able to find a motel to stay in until the closing day. I made up my mind that I would never return to Atlanta to live. I made enough money from the sale of my condo to use as a down payment on a house. I contacted a realtor I knew who specialized in houses, to help me find a house to buy.

We both knew this would take longer than a month to do. A motel would be too costly for me to stay that length of time, so I rented an apartment in a poorer area of Detroit, to save money, while we looked for the ideal house for me to buy. We found a showplace of a home in one of the more upscale neighborhoods in Oakland County. I used all of my money for the down payment.

I had made up in my mind I would never call my family again, because I felt they didn't care for me. I didn't give them my new address. Mom tried to get my new address from the Department of Social Security. They wrote me saying, "Your mother is trying to locate you; please contact her." I didn't respond to Social Security, nor did I contact my mother. It wasn't until 1995 I saw my family again (10 years later).

The voices I heard continued to haunt me. I was now writing down and keeping notes on everything I heard. I kept these notes for years, hoping the good things I wrote down would manifest. I began to talk to Rebecca, the astrologist I had met earlier for a reading. I became her godchild. She was of the Catholic faith, and introduced me to the Catholic Church. Being much older than me, and having no way to get around, I drove her to church every Sunday, until she convinced me to join the church. I became a Catholic. Rebecca and I went to church together until she could no longer attend. She was too sick.

I isolated myself again, because I had no choice. I had no close friends. Just to get some air, I took drives to the park, through neighborhoods or on the expressway, alone. Most of the time I couldn't keep my eyes opened as I drove. I wasn't getting adequate rest, because I was still stressed from living in Georgia.

I had several car accidents in one year. In one accident I broke my nose and had to have plastic surgery. To keep my license from being revoked, I had to attend a Driver's Training Class. I drove my car to get around until the motor died. I had no money to have it repaired. I had to take a taxi to the grocery store to buy groceries so I could eat.

I was low on money. I couldn't keep up my mortgage and my heat got shut off. I had to use a small electric heater for my bedroom. I had lived in this house for three years. Rather than lose the house, I put it up for sale. The president of a local bank, bought the house from me at a good price. When it was time for me to move out, he had to take legal means to make me move. I didn't know I needed help and he didn't know I was sick. I was hearing voices telling me "the house was still mine" and that "I was meant to have it." Hearing that, I made no effort to get out; but, legally the house was Mr. Harper's because we had closed on it.

Even though he had a hard time getting me out, I finally made up my mind I had to move. I bought another house in Southfield, Michigan where I lived for three years. This was also a nice house, but much smaller. I stayed there until I was foreclosed on by the owner for not keeping up my mortgage payments. At the same time, I lost eleven acres of land I had purchased long before in Upper Michigan.

I got behind in my mortgage because my disability payments were being wrongfully garnished by an attorney who took the money to pay off charge card debts I owed years before. Even though it was unlawful to garnish disability income, I didn't know how to stop this from happening to me. The bank didn't listen to me when I spoke to them, and I had no money to hire an attorney. So, the attorney garnished my monthly income almost every month. This left me with nothing in my bank account. Some months I would beat the garnishments before going through and withdraw my money from my account. When I didn't, I couldn't pay my mortgage nor eat.

I once had to search throughout places in my home where I thought I might find loose coins in order to buy food. One month I found enough coins to buy a box of macaroni. So, I ate nothing but plain macaroni for the whole month. I had no one I could call on for help. And I didn't know how to get state aid. Rebecca was in need herself, so she wasn't a help to me. I stayed inside the house all the time not knowing what to do.

There was a mouse in the house that would run across the floor while I sat quietly on the sofa or in a chair. This mouse seemed very tame because it ran from under the refrigerator every time I opened the door. This seemed very strange to me, and I became scared. I'm not sure if this was for real. I may have been seeing things.

I was so worn out from the years past, I slept real hard. I had dreams so real-like, vivid and in color, as if I was looking at a screen in a movie theatre. Every time I closed my eyes I dreamt. I felt like I had not slept at all the next day. I dreamt of things that sometimes happened. Once I dreamt that a mouse was dead in my kitchen sink covered with water. Weeks later, I actually saw this mouse dead in my kitchen sink with his eyes bucked, just like in the dream. This was scary because I knew of it before it happened. My nightmare had come true. I still can't explain this happening. Some say that people with a mental illness, like schizophrenia, can have a sixth sense. This may be true.

Eventually my lights were turned off in the house so I had to burn candles for light. I was evicted. The man who sold the house to me, had all of my belongings set out side. He had hired more than eight people through the court to set my belongings outside. The police were there. My inoperable car was placed on the street. People from all around the neighborhoods came to see what was happening. I was embarrassed. I had no place to go, so I slept in my car for the night. I was homeless. Luckily for me, the next day was a check day so I walked to the bank. I was able to withdraw all of my money before the garnishment order went in for that month. When I left to go to the bank, most of my belongings in the yard were stolen....the television, cameras, books, etc. I put all that was left in storage. I would have had to sleep in my car again, but God pulled me through. I found a low grade motel nearly four miles from the house.

I stayed there for a week until I found an apartment to move to. In the lobby of the motel I thought I saw a man who had worked with me, working at the clerk's desk in the motel. I kept my distance because I didn't want him to recognize me. Stress triggers delusions and hallucinations. I was seeing people that I thought I knew, even though it really wasn't them. Now I realize this clerk was not the man I knew before.

I bought a newspaper and looked up "apartments for rent". I answered an ad within walking distance of the motel. I went there, and the apartment manager rented the apartment to me without running a check. (I had poor credit, so I wasn't expecting to get it.) This was a blessing for me to get a place to stay in as quick as I did, and without a credit check.

I didn't know at that time that living alone again was not a good thing for me. I moved to the apartment that same week. I was given a unit in the back of the complex…..which was very quiet and secluded. I had to somehow move my belongings out of storage to the apartment. So I rented a small truck to take what was left of my belongings out of storage. I loaded the truck myself, and unloaded it without help. Somehow, I had an enormous amount of strength then. My car wasn't running, so I had to have it towed to the apartment parking lot. The garnishments had come to an end the month after I moved in, so I had enough money every month to keep up my rent, utilities, and enough to buy food. I didn't have enough money left over to have the car repaired, so I kept it parked on the apartment lot.

Rebecca and I had stopped communicating because she was placed in a nursing home, where she died. The few people I knew did not keep in touch with me, nor call me back even when I tried to talk to them. I felt rejected. I lost interest in everyone. I gave up on everybody – my family, and the people I knew. I made myself believe that I could live without anyone. If and when my telephone rang, I didn't answer it. I stayed in my apartment all day watching television, doing jigsaw puzzles or sewing. I had started back to drinking alcohol, this time heavily. The only time I got out of the apartment was to buy food. The food store was less than a mile from where I lived. I walked there sometimes and other times I took a taxi. I lived like this for five years. I had no social contact. No one visited me, and I very rarely bumped into a neighbor. I was still having the vivid movie-like dreams like before. I was still not on any psychotropic medications.

I enjoyed listening to voice(s). The voice(s) I heard in my head became all the company I wanted and needed. The majority of the time I listened to them giving me news about other people, and about what people had done to me. They also told me things to do and the benefits that would come out of it. Most times I obeyed them. I was once told to "walk to the grocery store and I would see Albert. Albert would give me some money to help me." Albert lived in California at the time. But, believing the voice I heard, I walked to the store. Sure enough, I saw him (or who I thought was him) standing in the checkout line like I was told. I left because I was afraid to say anything to this person.

During this time I also saw (or thought I saw) people I had known in New York, in Michigan, walking down the streets or in stores. I thought they were real but I was just hallucinating. I have had other instances where I thought the television talked to me, thinking that it was sending me messages and warnings. I once saw a TV commercial on guns. A gun was pointing directly at me on the screen. I thought this was a warning for me. I also thought I could control my microwave with my mind. I believed that I could turn it on with my mind, because one evening as I sat quietly, it did start up by itself, I thought.

Whenever I was in a store I thought the clerks were watching me to see if I would steal something, so I acted differently. A store manager once asked me if "something was wrong with me." I said "no" and left...not even buying what I was there for. I began to neglect my personal hygiene....sometimes for weeks. I didn't take a bath until I went out of the house to buy groceries.

Then I changed. After not bathing for a while, suddenly I became an extremely clean person. I just couldn't stop bathing. I couldn't stand to wear some clothing I had. I washed a piece of clothing every day, even if it was already clean. I couldn't stand for the clothing I had on to rub against anything in the apartment. I would take it off and spot wash it.

I continued to sleep a lot and dreamt as soon as I closed my eyes. I couldn't get out of bed. I had excruciating headaches. I was depressed, but I didn't feel like anything was wrong with me. I prayed a lot, read my Bible and listened to religious stations. I started to believe the one voice who talked to me the most was my guardian angel and that I was someone else.

I thought I was Jesus Christ. I still kept to myself and believed I was going through suffering like Jesus Christ because I had a tough life. I believed that I was suffering because I was carrying my cross. I spent many days sewing, making my own clothes. I felt Jesus made his own clothes, so I had to do the same. I even had the initials "JC" engraved on a pen and pencil set I ordered by mail.

It was now the year 1993, and I had not seen a psychiatrist since 1984. I made myself believe that hearing voices was a spiritual thing, which was good. I believed that I was gifted to hear them, because no one else could. My sense of smell heightened. I often smelled rubbing alcohol when none was around. I hadn't talked to anyone about myself since Dr. Charleston. This was my secret. I was content just keeping to myself and listening to the voices I heard in my head. I thought I had special powers.

During my last year (1995) in this apartment I flipped out. Mr. Thomas, who had allowed me to park my inoperable car on the lot died. We got a new manager. Mr. Fitzsimmons, the new manager asked me to have my car repaired or move it off the lot. I told him I would take care of it—but never did because I didn't have the money. He had the car impounded. I never saw my BMW again.

At the same time, I started getting notices from the office saying my rent was "past due." This "unpaid rent notice" was in error. My rent was being paid every month, and it was paid up-to-date. I had cancelled checks to show that it had been paid. In the process of trying to straighten this matter out, the office manager posted an eviction notice on my door.

I had one eviction before moving to this apartment, and I wasn't ready to have another one. This was too much for me to bear. I had a gun in the apartment. It was a 38 automatic, "Saturday Night

Special," so it's called. This is when a voice told me that afternoon that I could "shoot a gun," and I was "a reincarnation of Al Capone" and that I had "taught Adam to shoot a gun," "so pull the trigger."

I got extremely drunk. My blood alcohol level exceeded the legal limit (I was told later). I started to fire the gun inside the apartment. I had not planned to kill anyone....even though I was angry with the landlord, and I had talked myself out of killing myself. I barricaded myself in the apartment and shot inside only. I shot at the walls, lights and doors. I was in a second floor apartment --- meaning, I wasn't at street level to shoot anyone. Plus I wasn't trying to shoot anyone. Two men walking nearby heard the shots coming from my apartment. They called 911 to notify the police.

The SWAT Team came and surrounded the building. My telephone rang and rang but I didn't answer. When I did answer the phone, Mr. Fitzsimmons was on the other end. Before he said any more to me, I tried to tell him what the apartment office manager was doing to me, but I just couldn't get it out the right way. So I hung up the phone.

Someone got on a PA system, asking me to "stop shooting" and to "come outside." I was later told this, but I didn't hear them. After shooting for a while I left the gun upstairs in the apartment and walked down the stairs to the front entrance. I looked out the door when a bullet struck me in the left eye. I didn't know I was injured until I saw the blood soaking the shirt I wore. I was wearing glasses when the bullet hit me. The left lens was shattered by the bullet. The broken glass and bullet injured my eye. I did not have my gun in my hand when I was shot. (See reference newspaper article.)

I immediately came inside the building after being shot, and went back upstairs to my apartment. My first thought was to head for the bathroom to wash my eye. Then I went to the bedroom to change into a clean shirt. The police shot tear gas through the apartment window. It did not go off. The reports all say they got me to come out of the apartment with tear gas. If this were so, they would not have been able to enter the apartment themselves.

I had long stopped shooting and didn't have the gun when they entered my apartment. I had intentionally left my door unlocked for them to come in. I was in the bathroom, very calm, when five or six officers came inside. They pushed me around roughly....as if I was resisting arrest. I did not try to fight back. They pushed me on the living room floor, twisting my arms forcefully behind my back, and then handcuffed me. My right shoulder was fractured in the process and stayed sore for months.

The officer who fired his gun had me ride in his vehicle to take me to the hospital. He first started to take me directly to jail, but I told him I had been shot. He couldn't tell because I had cleaned up the blood and washed my eye out. I had no coat on and I was barefoot in the month of January. They didn't wait for me to get a coat nor shoes. They just took me.

An officer fired his gun. It was thought that I may have shot myself; and that a bullet may have ricocheted from my gun and hit me...but, I was standing at the building front entrance when a bullet from the outside hit me; and I had no gun in my hand at the time. (See reference newspaper article.)

He took me first to Southfield Regional Hospital to be treated. The doctors examined me in the Emergency Room to see if I was hurt on any other parts of my body. I had to take off all my clothes. As I was examined, the policemen were in and out the examining room. They gave me no privacy. I do remember thinking I was like Superman, because the bullet didn't kill me. And I spoke out to them that "kryptonite was the only thing that could kill me."

I wasn't talking with any sense at all. I was saying what a voice was telling me to say. I demanded that I be taken to another hospital a few miles away. This hospital is considered as one of the nations' leading medical centers. That's why I wanted to go there. The paramedics put me in an ambulance and drove me to that hospital.

That night, when I arrived at their Emergency Room, I was quite disappointed. I had to wait in an adjoining room, with an officer, because the waiting room was crowded. I waited in the room, sitting in a wheelchair, until the next morning before I was treated. All night

I sat in that wheelchair, with my wrists handcuffed with the Officer guarding me.

When I finally got a hospital bed, I was treated like a criminal. My ankle was shackled in chains to the bed and there were three officers always around. Two officers stayed in the hospital room with me and another one sat at the door as if I would run away. They only unchained my ankle from the bed when I had to go to the bathroom. My door was always kept open. I could see and hear people walking up and down the hall passing my room. Dr. John Houser and his staff were assigned to treat me. I had to have three operations on my left eye in the seven days I was there. Every time I was operated on, a police officer stood at the door of the operating room, guarding to make sure I didn't escape or make trouble. I may have been hallucinating, but I believe my doctor brought a shotgun with him in my hospital room one day.

I was resting one evening when a clerk from the courthouse and a sheriff came into my room. They had a manual typewriter with them. They arraigned me as I lay in my hospital bed. All the while in the hospital, I was still listening to voices, and seeing people I thought I knew. I thought I saw a man in a white suit with a beard pass my door. He looked like the real Colonel Sanders of KFC. I thought this was him. The voice told me he was "there for me…to help me get out of my situation." I waited for his help, but I never saw him again.

Dr. Houser was unable to save my eye. Presently, I wear a prosthetic left eye. I will always believe that I didn't receive the best service from the Hospital because of the circumstances under which I was admitted, and because of my attire. I had on no shoes and no coat in January. I had been drinking alcohol all day. My alcohol level content was extremely high. My hair was nappy and sticking up on my head, and I smelled like urine. I still don't know how the urine smell got on me because I did not urinate on myself. My clothes smelled like they had been sprayed with urine. I was handcuffed and escorted by a policeman. Had it not been for this, I feel I would have gotten better service.

Woman arraigned in standoff with police

BY MARGARET O'BRIEN
STAFF WRITER

COURTS

The Eccentric THURSDAY, JANUARY 26, 1996

Charged *from page 1A*

Standoff
from page 1A

Afternoon drama: *A Southfield officer equipped with special gear leaves the scene after a woman was apprehended following a standoff with police Friday.*

Part IV

MORE TROUBLES JAIL AND HOSPITALS

After being discharged from the hospital, I went to the Southfield Jail, in January, 1995 for two days. They put me in an overcrowded jail cell with people who were waiting to be sentenced by the Southfield Court like me. I had a polygraph and was fingerprinted while there. My hallucinating ran wild, believing what the voices were saying about the people there. I was seeing people who couldn't possibly have been there. I thought I saw my nephew, who was in Georgia at the time. No one could convince me that wasn't him.

Before my time to go before the Judge, I was taken out of jail, and waited in a room with white painted cement walls near the Courtroom. I had no place to sit but on a cement step on the floor and I had to use a toilet stool which was sitting open, with no walls around it, in the room. The room had a steel door which had a small window covered by bars. I waited alone in the room. I was so sleepy and tired; I slept on the cement step, which was meant to be for sitting.

It seemed like hours before I was called to go before the Judge. When I was finally called to go to the Courtroom, two police officers

escorted me there. I was in handcuffs. I remained quiet as the Judge
read the charges.

They were: "Discharge of Firearms in or at a Building." Defendant
did intentionally discharge a firearm in a facility that she knew or
had reason to believe was an occupied structure in reckless disregard
for the safety of another; contrary to the statute in such case made
and provided and against the peace and dignity of the People of the
State of Michigan.

"Malicious Destruction of Building over $100.00." Defendant
did willfully and maliciously destroy or injure a building or an
appurtenance thereof situated as an apartment building, resulting
in damage thereto, the value of which was in excess of $100.00;
Contrary to the statute in such case made and provided and against
the peace and dignity of the People of the State of Michigan.

"Felonious Assault." Defendant did make an assault with a
dangerous weapon, to-wit, a gun, but without intending to commit
the crime of murder or to inflict great bodily harm less than the
crime of murder; Contrary to the statute in such case made and
provided and against the peace and dignity of the People of the State
of Michigan.

All three charges resulted in a felony. I was charged with felonious
assault because I had gotten angry with a mail delivery man at my
apartment one day and waved my gun in his face. The delivery man
made a delivery to my apartment, and I noticed that the package
was slightly damaged at the corner of the box. He told me I "could
refuse the package and have the company send me another one." I
couldn't accept this. As he stood in the hallway at my door writing a
phone number down for me to call, he looked up and saw that I had
a gun in my hand, asking him "why had he opened my package". I
said, "this isn't the first time this has happened, and that I was "tired
of delivery services opening my packages." He again told me that I
"could refuse the package." I saw that he was wearing an earring
in his ear, so I asked him to take it off, waving the gun in his face. I
then told him to "leave the package and get the hell out of here." He
backed all the way down the stairway and left.

I had no intention of shooting him. I just wanted to scare him for delivering a package to me which was damaged. I had long forgotten about this incident, but this delivery man had not. He pressed charges against me after he learned of the shooting.

The Judge sentenced me to the Oakland County Jail. That night when I was transferred from the Southfield Jail, I was transported to Oakland County Jail with other inmates. The guards had us shackled in chains around the waist. We were guarded as we walked one behind the other in a line to a huge truck which transported us. The ride was a brief one coming from the Southfield Jail. When we arrived at the jailhouse, the guard had me place my hands above my head against the wall and had me straddle my legs as he searched me. He said to me, "you know what to do", as if I had gone through this before, but I didn't know. This was all new to me. He then gave me jailhouse clothes to change into.

Jeanie and mother, who were listed as my emergency contacts on the apartment contract, had been notified by the Southfield police. Jeanie informed them that I had seen Dr. Charleston in the past, and that I had problems with psychosis. She also told them the last thing I said to her before the incident, was that "someone is going to die." She thought she was helping. But this didn't help the situation at all. I did say this to her, but I didn't mean that I was going to kill someone. I said it because, in my head, I was told that my mother would die soon. I just wanted her to know this.

Jeanie and my brother-in-law came to visit me the week I was placed in the Oakland County Jail. They drove all the way from Georgia to the jail in a blizzard. Mom didn't come with them, but she called the jailhouse. The warden advised her of the incident, and that I had been shot. She was further advised that "the injury was not life threatening" and that "I had been treated in the hospital" and that I was under arrest. Mom apologized for my behavior and mentioned to him I had a mental problem.

Jeanie and Robert got to Michigan on a non-visitation day at the jail. Technically, they were not supposed to see me, but the warden allowed them to visit me regardless of the rule because they had made the effort and had come from so far away. I was under a $25,000 bail bond, and the only way I could get it was to have my sister and brother-in-law put their home up as bail. They wouldn't do this; therefore, I was in jail close to two months.

Being in jail is something I never want to relive again. The inmates were always guarded, meals were served at a certain time every day, and there was a time to watch TV and a time to turn in for the night. Added to this, I didn't care for my cellmate. We had our differences over many things. She slept on the bottom bunk in our jail cell so I had to take the top bunk. It was difficult for me to climb over her to get to my bunk. We even argued about the lights. Even though the cell was dark, and needed the lights on, she wanted to keep the lights off. I wanted to keep them on until we were told by the guard to turn them off. She did not want a cellmate. She told the guard that I "smelled" and she "wanted to move to another cell or move me out." Neither one of us moved. The guard made me shower, even though I had been showering every day. Even though Becky and I argued a lot, I tried not to engage in them because I didn't want to go to solitary confinement. The voices in my head continued to talk to me. One voice made me believe I had talked to Becky years before in downtown Pontiac. Sure enough, I thought I had seen her, but she could not recall seeing me before jail. I realize now that I was hallucinating. I had also dreamt long before that I would be in jail someday. This came true, because I was incarcerated. I can't explain this.

The medical assistance was another issue there. It wasn't the best. There were nurses there who came in on different shifts to put eye drops in my injured eye that Dr. Housen had prescribed for me. Most times it was not done on time or in a professional manner. They didn't care if I got the eye drops or not. It seemed to me that they weren't trained very well to handle an eye condition.

I still could see out of my right eye wearing my taped up glasses. I wasn't up to watching TV when we could, but before lockdown was called every night we could spend time in the sitting area to watch TV. The few times I went, I was cautioned about where to sit. The majority of the time, the women in the sitting room wanted to start a fight even if you sneezed, or looked at them in a different way. Most times I stayed in my jail cell and slept during TV hours. I didn't want to be bothered with anyone anyway. On Sundays, I went to religious service in the Jail Chapel. A different preacher would come in every Sunday to minister to us.

Every week we were given lotion, soap and toothpaste to use. We had to have our own money for extras, like candy bars or cigarettes. Jeanie had left me with spending money when they visited me, so I was able to buy candy. I had problems keeping my dry skin moisturized because the small bottle of lotion they gave us wasn't enough. At meal time, I hid and brought out packs of butter we got with our meals. I used the butter on my skin to prevent dryness.

The food was just like what I had heard about jailhouse food. It was dull and most of the time it was some kind of dried food. We had oatmeal every morning. I couldn't get accustomed to eating it. I did without most mornings.

Each inmate had a chore to do each day. The first week there, I was still healing from my eye wound, so I didn't get a chore to do. But, later, my chore was to clean the laundry room. I did this every evening after dinnertime until I was discharged.

I was evaluated by the Michigan Forensic Psychiatry and Psychology Center more than once while incarcerated to determine my competency to stand trial and criminal responsibility. I had to give my informed consent to a Forensic Psychiatry and Psychology Clinician for these evaluations to take place. The clinician introduced himself. He stated, "You have been ordered by the court to undergo an examination to determine your Competency and Criminal Responsibility. My purpose for talking with you is to complete an evaluation to determine your mental state and to answer any questions raised by the court." The clinician also said that "a report will be sent to the court detailing the clinical findings and stating an opinion. Additional testimony might be necessary and (he) may be required to tell the court what he observed and what I said. As a result of the interview, it might be necessary to request psychological testing, the results of which also might be disclosed in the report to the court or in the course of testimony." I was asked, "Do you understand what I have told you?" "Yes," I replied. I had to sign my name to a form consenting to what I had heard. They also gave me the Minnesota Multiphasic Personality Inventory Test.

The Forensic Psychiatry and Psychology Center was located in Southeastern Michigan. Each time I went there, (by court order), a sheriff deputy drove me there, in handcuffs. Sometimes I spent the whole day at the Forensic Center being evaluated. Then I had to return to the jailhouse. I stayed in the Oakland County Jail nearly two months before a verdict in my case was given.

The clinical psychologist/consulting forensic examiner from the Center contacted the Honor Judge of the Judicial District Court with his evaluation….. "This is the Forensic Psychiatry and Psychology Center referral of this 46-year-old divorced black female who was born in Laurens County Georgia. She is charged with Malicious Destruction of Property and Illegal Discharge of a Firearm in the Judicial District Court for Oakland County. The defendant was referred for evaluation of Competency to Stand Trial and Criminal Responsibility on separate Orders dated February 2, 1995 and signed by the Judge. Prior to the interview, the defendant was informed of the purpose of the evaluation, of the fact that a report would be issued according to legal requirements, and that the examiner might be subpoenaed to testify about the report or anything else related to the examination. Ms. B. Ruoss was evaluated at the Forensic Psychiatry and Psychology Center on February 21, 1995, in a clinical interview lasting two hours and 55 minutes. Administered also was psychological testing consisting of the Minnesota Multiphasic Personality Inventory-2 (MMPl-2). At that time, the defendant was in custody and was transported to the Center by Oakland County Sheriff's Deputies. She appeared for the evaluation dressed in relatively clean, jail-issued clothing. Her personal hygiene and grooming appeared adequate. Her hair was combed and pulled back behind her head. She wore glasses held together with masking tape. Noteworthy in her appearance was an injury to her left eye, apparently sustained in the course of the incident prompting the alleged offenses. The defendant's gait appeared normal and, other than a reduced activity level, her motor behavior was unremarkable. The defendant denied that she had received any prescription or nonprescription drugs or alcohol on the day of the evaluation. She remained alert and demonstrated no clouding of consciousness during the interview. She was oriented in all spheres as evidenced in her ability to correctly state her full name, age, and the date, place and general context of the evaluation. She interacted with the examiner in a calm, soft spoken manner and cooperated fully with evaluation procedures. Most noteworthy in the defendant's clinical presentation was evidence of a number of suspicious ideas reaching paranoid delusional proportions. She accused an unspecified person or persons of interfering with her attempts to maintain a stable financial and housing status. In a rambling manner, she reviewed her housing and financial problems over the previous ten years. She explained, "It seems like somebody has been pushin' me out of my houses." She described a series of evictions which she acknowledged were related in part to her own financial problems but which ultimately she attributed to illegal proceedings. She indicated that as recently as December of 1994, she received an eviction notice, with no legitimate basis, from her apartment in Southfield, her residence at the time of her arrest on the instant charges. She indicated that while living in her Southfield apartment her car had been vandalized. She explained that her tires had been slashed and a decorative symbol had been removed. She also indicated that many pieces of mail and parcels delivered to her home had been opened and resealed. She indicated that she did not know who was intercepting her mail or why. The defendant also described herself as suffering from unusual illnesses at her various homes in Michigan, including her apartment in Southfield. For example, she stated at one of her homes she developed almost continuous diarrhea. She described herself as more recently suffering from a "different kind of sickness" which seemed to result in her falling asleep at unusual times and for long periods. She implied, but did not make a specific accusation, that these illnesses were the result of a purposeful attempt by someone to infect her. She noted repeatedly that "nobody is looking into this." She indicated that she had been in and out of court regarding her housing problems and that "the court should recognize this as a problem that should be dealt with." When questioned specifically regarding other types of delusional ideas, the defendant also described déjà vu type experiences and a past belief that people could read her mind or that she could mentally influence the behavior of others. In addition to these irrational beliefs, the defendant also reported that she was experiencing ongoing auditory hallucinations, even during the forensic interview. She was somewhat vague and perhaps evasive in describing these experiences. She noted that the voices sounded like "different people" whom she did not know. She indicated that she could not figure out what the voices were saying to her. She indicated that although she was experiencing auditory hallucinations, she was nevertheless concentrating on the forensic interview. This was consistent with interview observations that she did not appear to be highly distractible and generally remained focused on the issue at hand. However, she frequently exhibited an unusual interjection as she spoke which sounded something like the word "mhm" which may have represented a concomitant or response to hallucinated voices. Mild cognitive slippage was indicated in her intermittently irrelevant and tangential speech. She did not display, however, a full-blown thought disorder. Her emotional responses were rather blunted in range and intensity but at all times consistent with the content of her speech. Indeed, she described her current mood as "neutral" and commented that, in the jail, she was "goin" along with the program." She denied or did not exhibit significant symptoms of a mood disturbance, including elated, irritable or depressed mood, sleep or appetite disturbance, behavioral hyperactivity, grandiose self-appraisal, or suicidal thoughts or plans. Her conversational style and working vocabulary suggested functional intellectual skills in the low average range. Formal mental status testing was not accomplished. Regarding pertinent medical information, aside from the above described vague, unusual illnesses she felt she had contracted over the last ten years in her various homes, she did not report any standard illnesses or diseases such as diabetes, hypertension or seizure disorder. She denied that she had ever sustained a serious head injury. Regarding pertinent mental health history, the defendant noted that she first sought mental health treatment from an outpatient psychiatrist when she moved to Michigan over ten years ago.

She indicated that this psychiatrist prescribed her psychotropic medications including Stelazine (an antipsychotic) and recommended her first and only psychiatric hospitalization at St Mary's Hospital in 1978. When asked if she thought she was experiencing any emotional problems, she initially asked what the examiner meant and then stated, "No more than just tired of where I'm gonna go (to live) next." Given her slow completion of the test, administration of the MMPi-2 was discontinued after #370. However, test results based on her completion of approximately two-thirds of the test was consistent with interview observations of a mental disorder in the paranoid spectrum, likely to be psychotic in proportions. In summary, Ms. Ruoss presented as a 46-year-old, divorced black female who appeared to be experiencing active symptoms of a mental illness in the paranoid spectrum. Her primary symptoms included auditory hallucinations, mild cognitive slippage, and paranoid ideation of delusional proportions. It appears that she has maintained a schizoid i.e., socially isolated lifestyle for many years. Concerning the issue of competency to stand trial, the law indicates that, "A defendant to a criminal charge shall be presumed to be competent to stand trial. He shall be determined incompetent to Stand Trial only if he is incapable because of his mental condition of understanding the nature and object of the proceedings against him or assisting in his defense in a rational manner." The defendant appeared generally aware of her current status as a defendant awaiting trial on charges she identified as "firin' a gun" and "damaging an apartment building." Although she indicated that she understood that charges could result in a prison sentence or fine or both, she appeared to minimize the seriousness of her legal situation in part as a result of to her current mental illness. As noted elsewhere in this report, the defendant appeared to be of low average intelligence and therefore capable of grasping relevant legal concepts and procedures. Questioning along these lines supported this conclusion. For example, the defendant indicated that the role of the judge was to "listen to the situation and make a decision" as to "guilty or not guilty." It was in the context of the defendant's ability to rationally assist counsel that serious competency concerns primarily emerged. The defendant did know the name of her attorney and understood his role as an advocate. She also was able to provide a generally coherent account of events associated with the alleged offenses. However, her mental illness appeared to be significantly interfering with her ability to rationally plan for her defense. Although the defendant did not categorically rule out the possibility of an insanity defense, she appeared to possess no insight into her mental condition. She appeared preoccupied with pursuing in court her own agenda of exposing harassment regarding her housing situation over the last ten years. Although she appeared, at one point, amenable to the possibility of a plea bargain if advised to take one by defense counsel, she later indicated that she would consider pleading guilty "as long as you don't hold me to it." In several other ways, she demonstrated impaired reasoning in the context of discussion of her defense options.

Therefore, as a result of an active mental illness, the defendant did not appear capable of rationally assisting counsel. It is the recommendation of this examiner that she be adjudicated incompetent to stand trial. It is further this examiner's opinion that the defendant, if provided appropriate treatment in a structured, inpatient, hospital setting, could be expected to regain competency within the time period provided by statute. Given the defendant's mental condition on this date, the criminal responsibility evaluation is being deferred. Should such an evaluation be desired after the defendant regains competency at a later date, it is requested that a new criminal responsibility be ordered and forwarded to the center. .... P. Wesley Clinical Psychologist/ Consulting Examiner"

The Director for the Forensic Psychiatry and Psychology Center followed up with the Judge of the Judicial District Court having this to say: "Ms. B. Ruoss, the defendant has been recommended Incompetent to Stand Trial. In accordance with the State of Michigan, Department Health Administrative Rules, the defendant has been evaluated by the Forensic Psychiatry and Psychology Center in regard to appropriate placement. In accordance with the evaluation, and in the event that the court determines that the defendant is Incompetent to Stand Trial and the Department of Mental Health is named the Medical Supervisor of Treatment, It is the recommendation of the Forensic Psychiatry and Psychology Center that the defendant be treated at Clinton Valley Center. .... Gary Wheeler Director"

In March, 1995, I was admitted to Clinton Valley Center Psychiatric Hospital on an "Incompetent to Stand Trial" order.

I was transported to the hospital by a sheriff deputy in his car, again in handcuffs. As soon as I was admitted I was examined by the doctors. They prescribed Haldol with Cogentin for my symptoms.

Part V

A PATIENT IN THE LOONEY BIN

Clinton Valley Center had a cold and lonely atmosphere. The exterior of the building reminded me of a castle in a storybook. It was located in a heavily-wooded setting. The inside had florescent ceiling lights and tile floors. The building was many small buildings joined by tunnels used for hallways. To get from one building to the other, you had to walk through a tunnel. My room was in the Meadowview 3 Building. I had this room to myself most of my time spent there.

We did have outings such as to the zoo, fairs, shopping, etc. Only those with special privileges were allowed to go off the premises. Occasionally, I spent supervised outdoor time to get some sun and to be outside. I only went shopping a few times with a supervised group, near the end of my stay there. I got my hair done by a beautician in the building who became somewhat of a friend. Susan kept my hair up. She always came to my room when the time came for her to do my hair.

We had indoor activities every day, like coloring, working jigsaw puzzles and cooking classes. The staff liked to see us busy and not sitting in the sitting room asleep. Every Fourth of July or Memorial Day, we had a picnic in the yard. We had grilled foods and all.

I was never content with anything I did there, because my mind was occupied with leaving and moving into an apartment on my own again. I didn't have any clothes with me except the ones I wore in, and a used dress, light coat and pants gotten from the hospital's closet. I wore these until I met Deloris. Deloris worked for Clinton Valley Center and she befriended me. Much to my surprise one day, she brought in a bag full of clothes just for me. The bag had a coat in it, because I didn't have a warm coat to wear. She sometimes would bring me cake to eat from her kitchen at home, just so I would have something different to eat. We are still friends and she still calls me to this day.

Another staff member was also concerned about me...a nurse. She was not too pleased that I was still wearing glasses held together by tape and that my blind eye was disfigured. She made sure that I got new glasses. She also took me to a Prosthetic Eye Doctor who made an artificial eye for my blind eye. I am still grateful for her help. The prosthetic changed my whole appearance. It is impossible for someone to see that I am blind in my left eye.

The Haldol didn't stop the voices altogether. The Haldol kept me so restless; it was hard for me to sit in one place for any length of time. I had to move around. In order to prevent this, I slept a lot. The staff didn't like this, but I couldn't help myself. I didn't tell my psychiatrist about this, for fear of being prescribed a medication with much worse side effects. I didn't want to take any meds. One night I was caught throwing my pills in the trash can. From then on, I was given Haldol injections with Cogentin once a month in my rear end.

The longer I stayed on the meds, the voices became less and less, but I could still hear talking in my head when I listened hard enough. I continued to believe what the voices told me. The voices told me I would be discharged soon. I looked out the window in the sitting room every day waiting for someone (whom I didn't know) to come and take me away from the place. I waited and waited, but the days turned into years.

I kept very quiet most of the time. I avoided talking to the other patients. This was my rebellion because I wanted to leave the hospital. Much worse, there were always fights among some of the patients – over what television channel to watch or who would sit in the most comfortable chair. I avoided them by doing things that would not cause trouble. I did not talk for a long time but when I did talk my throat was often sore.

I did not stop going to court and being evaluated by the Forensic Psychiatry and Psychology Center while at this hospital. A Clinton Valley Center employee, along with a sheriff deputy would escort me there, handcuffed, in a squad car. On one occasion, Deloris was the employee who went with me to court. She kept quiet the whole time, on the way there and in court. The judge did not release me that time. I was sent back to Clinton Valley Hospital. Deloris was just as disappointed as I was, as she was hoping that I be released as well.

I really didn't have a fair chance before the judge anyway. I was never allowed to say anything. Furthermore, before going in the courtroom, I was always assigned a court appointed attorney to represent me - someone I had never met until the day of court and who was never the same attorney I had in past hearings. This wasn't good for me, because none of the attorneys were with me long enough to hear my story to justly defend me.

Each time before being called into the courtroom, I sat in a small locked room with a barred window on the door. The court appointed attorney did not even come into the room to discuss my case. He spoke to me through the small window on the door only giving me his name. None of the attorneys who represented me in court showed interest in my case. Therefore, the many times I was in court, was not to my favor. The judge's verdict was never a discharge.

While still at Clinton Valley Hospital, I received a court order requesting that I be moved to the Forensic Psychiatry and Psychology Center in Southeastern Michigan on a 90-day or longer intervention plan for further evaluations and treatment. I packed up my few belongings and moved to the Forensic Center in December, 1996. I was there until July, 1997. When I first arrived I was placed on a wing separate from the others in the building. I had my own private room; it was somewhat like being in a jail cell. Later in my stay I was in a room with other women. I met with the chief clinician and the unit psychiatrist as soon as I arrived there.

They documented my admission actions, recounting the offense as reported to them ………. "Ms. Ruoss had a handgun and was observed shooting from a second floor window. When officers arrived, they heard shots fired from within the building and also heard a woman scream. After hearing more shots, officers observed a black female with a gun. Attempts were made to speak with the woman by public address system and via telephone. She did not speak to the officers. Gunshots were exchanged and Ms. Ruoss was shot in the left eye. Teargas was lobbed into the building and Ms. Ruoss was apprehended. She was yelling that she was "being saved, it was the end, and it was time to be resurrected." Ms. Ruoss stated that she was "Jesus Christ" and that she was in "resurrection." Reports indicate that, at the time of the incident, Ms. Ruoss was hallucinating. In the examiner's opinion, during the time in question, that Ms. Ruoss had a psychotic interpretation of her experience and, due to her delusional beliefs that she was in mortal danger, behaved in a way that she saw as being self-protective. As such it is the opinion of the examiner that, at the time of the alleged offense, Ms. Ruoss was not responsible for her actions. It is the opinion of the examiner, that a finding of not guilty by reason of insanity is appropriate. Ms. Ruoss reported a long psychiatric history including outpatient treatment which started around 1971. After her two-week hospitalization at St Mary's Hospital in 1978, she received no psychiatric treatment until the above noted incident. During her stay at St Mary's Hospital, reports indicate that she had both hallucinations and delusions. At the time of her admission to Clinton Valley Hospital March, 1995, it was clear that she was responding to auditory hallucinations and was quite preoccupied. In summary, Ms. Ruoss appears to be a female who has had a long history of mental illness, however, was untreated for many years after her private psychiatrist retired in 1984 and this was when she stopped taking medications. She lived a very isolative lifestyle and was unemployed and became increasingly paranoid about others' intentions and would misperceive reality. She appears to lack insight into her mental illness in regards to the crime she committed." "During this interview, she seemed to discount the seriousness of the alleged incident and was mainly concerned with how long she would have to stay at the Forensic Psychiatry and Psychology Center and appeared upset that the police officers had injured her eye. When informed that most likely she would be supervised by the NGRI Committee for many years to come, she did not seem to like hearing this information and she wanted to move out of state to join her family, her mother and siblings in Georgia. She appears to be in good remission of psychotic symptoms at this time (01/02/97) as she denies having any auditory or visual hallucinations and appears to be in fair contact with reality. Plans are for her to continue her current antipsychotic medications as well as receive individual supportive psychotherapy. Her mental status will be monitored and her behavior will be observed to further assess her current level of functioning and to determine the extent to which her previous thought disorder still persists. .... Donald McKenna Unit Psychiatrist/Chief Clinician"

The Forensic Psychiatry and Psychology Center wasn't the most desirable place to be. I do remember there was a small sitting room with a television where the patients gathered. The kitchen was on the same wing. The only people I saw were the patients, as well as staff and doctors. There was no outside contact and no visitors.

Since it was around Christmas when I arrived, there was a Christmas tree near the sitting room. On Christmas Day we received gifts...something we could use in the hospital. I was given a pair of socks.

There were classes on medication management and indoor activities like exercising, bingo and music. We went outside occasionally. You needed your own money to make telephone calls, using the coin-operated phone. Mother had sent me money in the mail when she wrote me, therefore I was able to call out.

I was unaware that, during my stay at the Forensic Center, <u>every</u> move I made there was monitored. I became knowledgeable of this after requesting my hospital records for use in writing this book. The staff, made up of a physician, social worker, psychologist, nurse, security, adjunctive therapist and dietitian, kept multidisciplinary progress notes on me from the time I was admitted up to my discharge. The notes were on how I slept during the night; when I got up to use the restroom; if I was cooperative in taking my medications; eating habits and how pleasant and cooperative I was and much more. Overall the notes always indicated that I was" nice and pleasant, very quiet, soft spoken, cooperative, had good hygiene, friendly to everyone; speaks when spoken to (but very seldom strikes up a conversation); very little socializing; attended some groups and classes sporadically (my attention wandered during class and needed to be re-directed); appetite good; smiled frequently but the affect was flat; denied hearing voices; isolative, with minimal interactions with staff and peers; hesitantly admits to having a mental problem; is guarded and makes limited eye contact; had difficulty in comprehending the legal situation she was in; voiced no complaints or concerns........I made an effort to be a good patient during my stay at the Forensic Center because I wanted to be released.

I stayed very depressed most of my adult life, but none of the psychiatrists recognized this until 2010 when I was hospitalized at Mt Pleasant General Hospital (I will discuss this later in the book). I stayed in bed most of the time at the Forensic Center and the doctors didn't stop me from doing so. I was discharged from the Forensic Center in July, 1997. I was still on the Haldol Decanoate 200 mg-IM every four weeks. I thought I would be allowed to go home after being discharged from the Center, but I had to return to Clinton Valley Hospital. The Chief Clinician from the Forensic Psychiatry and Psychology Center issued my Discharge Papers...The charges against me were listed in the summary and what had happened in January, 1995. My course of treatment at the Forensic Psychiatry and Psychology Center was that I was seen for psychotherapy sessions on a weekly basis with a chief clinician. I received nursing care as well as supervision and a milieu treatment program on the women's unit where I resided. I was an active member of the activity therapy program as well as church and gym which were housed off the unit. I enjoyed music therapy which was on the unit. The clinician reported "Ms. Ruoss responded favorably to treatment and during clinical sessions she has shown some insight into her mental illness, stating that she needs to stay on her medications as it has taken away the voices and helps to keep her stable. She has behaved very well on the women's unit, getting along with others. However, she is somewhat shy and does not socialize much with peers or staff on the unit. However, she has been an excellent patient as she is always polite, well-behaved and cooperative. She is very high functioning and attends activity therapy where she participates in music, movies, cooking, and music therapy and exercise class. She takes care of her personal needs as well as maintaining excellent grooming and hygiene. She has behaved excellently during her time at the Forensic Center and there have been no significant behavioral problems noted on her part. At this time, she appears to be stable. She is taking medications to control psychotic symptoms and reports no delusionary thought or auditory hallucinations at this time. It appears that she could return to Clinton Valley Center where she was placed during the past year on an IST order. It is my recommendation that she be involved in active treatment programming such as symptom management classes, work therapy programs, activity therapy programs, and individual counseling sessions where she can continue to work on understanding the symptoms and behavior that led her to become incarcerated. It is also recommended that she be followed by Community Mental Health on an ongoing basis for an indefinite period of time upon release from Clinton Valley Center. The possibility of transferring her case down the road to Georgia where her mother and sister reside should be considered as they would provide family support to her as she currently has no family in the immediate area. Diagnostic impression: Schizophrenia, Paranoid Type." .... Donald McKenna Chief Clinician

I moved back to Clinton Valley Psychiatric Hospital, living the same regimen as before. I wasn't released from Clinton Valley Hospital as I had thought. Word was around that "the hospital was getting ready to shut down." Before Clinton Valley closed its doors for good, I was transferred to Northville Psychiatric Hospital in Northville, Michigan. Before I left for Northville Hospital I had another Forensic Evaluation. This was regarding my Criminal Responsibility. I was evaluated by the Forensic Psychiatry and Psychology examiner in September, 1997. The examiner wrote a letter to the Prosecuting Attorney of the District Court with this to say. "It is quite clear that Ms. Ruoss was not only mentally ill at the time of her alleged offense but also was either not able to or willing to share her then ongoing experience with this examiner due to the continued presence of symptomatic indications of her disorder. After reviewing all information available to this examiner, it is the opinion that, at the time of the alleged offense, Ms. Ruoss was not only mentally ill but also, due to her delusional thinking, unable to recognize the wrongfulness of her actions. It is the examiner's opinion that during the time in question, she had a psychotic interpretation of her experience and, due to her delusional beliefs that she was in mortal danger, behaved in a way that she saw as been self-protective. With this being, it is my opinion that, at the time of the alleged offense, Ms. Ruoss was not responsible for her actions. As such, it is my opinion, Ms. Ruoss be found of not guilty by reason of insanity." .... Lawrence Tisdale Assistant Director, Evaluation Unit Consulting Examiner

Northville Psychiatric Hospital was like an old-fashioned asylum. It had high ceilings, cement walls and cement floors. The windows in the bedrooms were so high from the floor, you could not see out of them when standing up. The beds were made of iron. There were four or more beds in each room. The beds were positioned side-by-side in a row. I was in a room with four people when I was admitted. By the time I was discharged, I was in a room with eight ladies. We each had our own locker in the room for clothes and personal items.

We also had a steel night stand next to each bed. There were no chairs in the patients' rooms.

The TV sitting room was where we sat to, color, work puzzles, converse and watch TV. We were not allowed in our bedrooms after breakfast except for a one hour nap each day after lunch. Afterwards we had to stay in the sitting room until bedtime at 8:00 p.m. Some evenings after dinner, we were allowed to go outdoors for a few minutes with supervision. The next morning we were up at 6:00 a.m., took our showers and went to breakfast.

Meds were passed out two times a day… mornings and evenings. The lines were always long at medication time. I would always dread having to wait in line to get my medications. I was prescribed Zyprexa over Haldol here at Northville Hospital. I can't remember why. Zyprexa worked until I developed the worst side effect from it that one could get. I became a borderline diabetic.

Dr. Habersham, my psychiatrist, felt I was overweight and by being so close to diabetic, he changed my meds from Zyprexa to Seroquel twice a day. It didn't stop the voices, and I didn't care. I thought the voices were helping me. Seroquel kept me sedated like a zombie, hungry all the time, and sleepy, like other meds I had taken. I did not allow myself to tell my psychiatrist about the voices nor the side effects. I just lived with it. I didn't realize then how important it is to talk to doctors and nurses until later in my illness.

I still had to go to Pontiac to appear in Court. Like always, I was transported handcuffed and rode in a police car driven by a sheriff deputy. I always had to return back to the hospital to stay…by the sheriff deputy.

I had the opportunity to work a paying job during my stay in Northville Hospital. The hospital packaged small automotive parts inside the hospital for automotive factories. I was asked by staff if I wanted to work and I said "yes." I knew then I was in the hospital for the "long haul" based on the Court's decisions. I worked daily from morning till noon except Saturdays and Sundays for two years, packaging small auto parts. This included packaging automobile plates, nuts, bolts, screws, etc. I made the hourly minimum wage.

When I got a paycheck, I deposited most of my money in the Hospital's Bank inside the hospital. I also earned my privileges to go on outings. I was allowed to go on field trips, in a supervised group. When we went shopping I bought personal items that I needed, and gifts at Christmas time. Everybody got gifts from the hospital at Christmas. The patients could also give each other gifts if they wanted to.

I had become friends with Shirley, who was in the same room with me. One Christmas she surprised me with a tube of my favorite color lipstick. I gave her a scarf. Shirley was there before I was admitted, and still there when I was discharged. We stayed friends while I was hospitalized. Back then (1990's) wasn't like today. Today you stay on a hospital's psychiatric ward two weeks to one month to stabilize you on medication(s), and then you are discharged.

I worked very hard on my job at the hospital, even though I had trouble keeping awake. With the money I earned, I was able to buy a 4" battery operated color television to watch, rather than use the sitting room to watch TV. When everyone was sleeping at night, I turned on my TV in bed, plugged in my earphones, and watched it under my bed covers. The nurses on the night shift never found out. If they had, my TV would have been confiscated.

I was discharged from Northville Psychiatric Hospital in March, 2000. A year before leaving, Dr. Woolfolk, at the hospital, evaluated me, and said, "You never make any trouble around here." That's when I had the courage to ask him "if I could be released." He replied, "Do you feel that you are ready?" I said "yes." I never talked to him again, but I was released from the hospital a year later after going to Court. It took them a whole year to do whatever they had to do to recognize I could leave. I had spent a total of five years in three psychiatric hospitals...Clinton Valley Center, The Forensic Psychiatry and Psychology Center and Northville Psychiatric Hospital. I was discharged on a ten year NGRI (Not Guilty by Reasons of Insanity) status, with restrictions that I couldn't leave the country for ten years, and I couldn't travel outside of Michigan without supervision.

I was assigned Court Appointed Attorney Atkinson to see that I adhere to this. Mrs. Irwin, my social worker from Northville Psychiatric Hospital was responsible for finding a place for me to stay. I was disappointed because I wanted to move into my own apartment, but the court had me go to a group home under a law similar to "Kevin's Law." Mrs. Irwin was very helpful. She made sure I would be satisfied with my new home. She showed me three group homes, and I had to choose the one I liked. I chose R & K Group Home in Southfield, MI owned by Mrs. William, because I could have my own private room.

Part VI

MORE HOSPITALS, THEN A LIGHT
AT THE END OF THE TUNNEL

As soon as I moved into the group home, Mrs. Sherwood, an employee from Easterseals Michigan, met me there. She was a Case Manager assigned to work with me. She scheduled me to see a psychiatrist at Easterseals in order to continue on my medication. She visited me every week to see how I was coming along. Living in a group home was quite a change for me as most of my life I had lived alone, and was independent.

At the home we had rules, but this was much better than being in a Psychiatric Hospital. We had to be in bed the same time every night and rise early the next morning. I volunteered to wash dishes after dinner which became my chore. And we, all five women, pitched in to clean the house on weekends.

During the day, we had to attend a day program at My Place Center for Wellness (formerly South Oakland Drop In Center.) Mrs. Williams drove us there in the morning and brought us home in the evening, five days a week. At the center we played card games, pool, did arts and crafts and watched TV. There were computers there, too. I spent most of my time on the computer as long as I stayed awake.

I was still having the same side effects from Seroquel as before. I may have acted strange sometimes, but this was not uncommon for someone living in a group home. I had to get used to it.

According to Mrs. Williams, I was one of the better house members to deal with. I did have more privileges. I met a man while living there. We usually went out to dinner. Mrs. Williams allowed me to visit him on weekends, as long as I was in by 11:00 p.m. Deloris, who befriended me while at Clinton Valley Hospital, came to visit me at the home also. We went out together. She was like family to me.

Being under restrictions by the Court, I couldn't fly to Georgia alone to see my family. Jeanie and my brother-in-law came to visit me, and I flew back to Georgia with them. Mrs. Williams allowed me to stay a month. Jeanie and Robert had to fly me back to Michigan when I was ready to return.

Attorney Atkinson visited me at the group home regularly. Unlike the other court appointed attorneys I had in the past, he showed great concern for me. He was one who listened to me. After being at the home a little into my second year, he had the restrictions lifted which the court had me under. I could now travel outside of Michigan alone, and I was allowed to leave the country if I wanted to. I was supposed to have eight more years under the NGRI restrictions, but now they were lifted.

I no longer had a criminal record. Everything was going in my favor. The caregiver at the home was concerned because I had not heard from Samuel since the 70's. "After all," she said, "he was your husband." "Is he still alive?" "Don't you want to know?" She wanted me to contact him. That's when I got on the computer and tracked him down. I gave him a call. He was living in Oklahoma and doing fine. I wished him well and never heard from him again.

I moved out of the group home within two years. God was on my side again, because, in my second year at the home, Easterseals launched a program to assist those ready to move out of group homes into homes of their own. Mrs. Sherwood, my psychiatrist, and Mrs. Williams felt that I was ready to leave and to live alone.

I was still hearing voices at times, but I never got out of line. I kept to myself. My schizophrenia can be described as having two minds. "One mind can listen to voices in my head and react to what I hear. The other mind sees things as they really are." I could deal logically with things...I felt.

Easterseals helped find me an apartment, gave me furniture from their resources and helped move me to Southfield. I can never forget how helpful Mrs. Sherwood was. She gave me dishes and silverware from her own home. She even moved my belongings from the group home in a van they had rented. She jokes with me today about how much stuff I had accumulated at the group home. I had help from Easterseals from start to finish. If not for them, I don't know what I would have done without their support and help in getting me started again. I would probably still be in a group home if it weren't for them.

I moved to my apartment the end of December, 2002. I continued to see my psychiatrist at Easterseals. I was assigned a different Case Manager, Ms. Carswell, because Mrs. Sherwood only dealt with clients in group homes. My new case manager made sure I got my prescriptions filled and that I saw my psychiatrist on time while in my new home. She also made visits to me. Easterseals was still there helping me.

I had never had this problem when I lived alone before, but every now and then, I can't sleep in a dark house. I have to keep a light on because I am afraid to be in the dark. My therapist, Eleanor, who I see today, says, "I am afraid because I have no one in the house with me." For a while I had lived with someone around me. The dogs had lived with me; in the group home there were others; in the hospitals I was always around others. Now I am in an apartment living alone. That's why I sleep with a lamp on in my bedroom. I have to get adjusted to no one living with me.

Deloris was the only friend I had, so we did a lot of things together. She called me when she wanted to go shopping or out to eat. She styled my hair for me, and she kept in touch with me. We even gave each other birthday gifts and exchanged gifts at Christmas time.

I stopped taking my meds because I felt that I was doing fine and didn't need them. In 2003, I enrolled at Siena Heights University to earn my Master's Degree. I had no car, so I took the bus to class in the evenings and a taxi back home around midnight three nights a week. I completed one quarter, but I was under a lot of stress in doing so.

I started to react to the voices in my head. While on a visit to Easterseals to see Ms. Carswell, she noticed a change in me. I was very argumentative with her for no reason. She recognized immediately that I wasn't taking my meds. She called an ambulance and had me admitted to Detroit Metro Psychiatric Hospital in March, 2003. The Admission Note/Mental Status were drawn up as soon as I got there......"Ms. Ruoss is a 54-year-old single black female. She was sent here from Easterseals where she was evaluated by her psychiatrist. It was stated her therapist filed a petition stating that she had been talking bizarre and illogically, and totally nonsensical. She is severely agitated; very bizarre and preoccupied. She is not taking her medications. When she decompensates she becomes acutely psychotic and behaves in a very dangerous manner, which happened in the past when she was living in an apartment in 1995 where she became very paranoid. She is also preoccupied and very illogical. She showed several bags of medicine that she had brought with her, 15 or more; some of them had prescriptions and others are herbal medicines. I am not sure how she was taking these, but she was not taking the Seroquel she was prescribed from Easterseals. She is extremely paranoid and is unable to be reasoned with. She has had several hospitalizations. She was released to a group home in 2000 which she subsequently left and ended up being serviced by Easterseals. She is uncooperative and preoccupied. From the moment she walked into the hospital she has been ready to leave. She is unable to sit and talk about what has been happening. The patient has very poor insight and judgment. She is acutely psychotic. She will be given Seroquel 200 mg g.h.s. She is considered a person who can potentially be a danger to herself with her violent behavior in the past, by acting in very highly unpredictable and dangerous manner. She had numerous herbal medicines that need to be investigated by the medical doctor when she has her physical examination. Continue close observation on the unit is recommended. The patient's social worker will get more information on her from Easterseals. At this time, the examiner was unable to determine prognosis. The estimated length of stay at hospital is one to two weeks. Diagnosis: Schizophrenia, Paranoid, with acute exacerbation; possible history of hypertension, arthritis, GERD and allergies. .... K. Brent, M.D."

The doctor wanted to give me Haldol injections because I would not take the Seroquel. I didn't think I was sick, so I refused to take any medication while there. I tried to convince the doctors that the supplements I was taking were all that I needed. They didn't accept this. After I refused to take meds for a few days while there, my refusal was no longer permitted. On 03/26/03 three nurses held me on my bed, while one injected me with a syringe full of Haldol in my rear end. From then on I received Haldol by injection.

Detroit Metro Psychiatric Hospital was a very small hospital. There were activities indoors and TV watching time. I never went outside on the enclosed patio they had there. Nor did I feel up to taking part in activities. All I wanted to do was leave and go back to my apartment, because I had responsibilities there. I couldn't notify my folks because I wasn't talking to them again. In my mind, I believed they were not related to me and they were stealing from me. How, I don't know. It was the voices speaking to me again.

Much like the Forensic Psychiatry and Psychology Hospital, Detroit Metro Psychiatric Hospital staff kept daily Progress Notes on me. Below are some of their findings:

03/20/03 -- "Ms. Ruoss, a 54 year old African American female, continues to be very paranoid, delusional, bizarre and very isolated. She tends to say that she has never had a mental illness and she was never seen. She continues to be responding to herself, talking and mumbling to herself. She refuses to take the medicines, and continues to be very preoccupied with wanting to be discharged. She met the court-appointed attorney. She has a court hearing scheduled for 03/24/03." .... K. Brent, M.D.

03/21/03 – "She continues to be very paranoid, delusional and guarded. She has been wearing the same clothes every day. She is very isolated, not interacting with people. She is very preoccupied about how she does not need medicines. She now talks about how she was in the hospital and NGRI, that there is nothing wrong with her, that there has never been, and that she is not having problems. There has been little contact with her family. She tends to believe her family is not her real family. There is no socialization and no friends. She has no goal-oriented focus. She is very paranoid and fixated on her delusions. Two caseworkers from Easter seals came and saw the patient. Apparently Easterseals has been quite concerned about her decompensation and potential psychotic decompensation." .... K. Brent, M.D.

03/25/03 – "Today the patient continues to be bizarre and illogical. She is preoccupied about the court being the one that gave her the Haldol injection. She also states that the court told her that all she needs to take is Haldol injections and she does not need to take any other medications. She has been refusing to take the Seroquel and she continues to be paranoid and fixated and constantly argues about things that she is preoccupied with. Last night she refused to take Seroquel. At this time, because of her constant refusal to take Haldol and Seroquel, I tried to persuade her to take them. She was laughing to herself and was preoccupied, responding to internal stimuli in her room while she was sitting there along with no one there. She still has on the same clothes." .... K. Brent, M.D.

03/26/03 – "Patient continues to be paranoid, delusional and bizarre. She has been refusing to take Seroquel, and because the patient is under court order at this time Haldol 5 mg was ordered. She was given a Haldol Deaconate injection, and she stated that those medicines do not agree with her, and they cause problems for her. The social worker will contact case management from Easterseals' ACT program. Discharge plans are to be discussed." ....K. Brent, M.D.

03/27/03 – "Today she continues to be paranoid, suspicious, bizarre and delusional. Last night she did not take the Seroquel as prescribed, and she ended up taking the Haldol injection 5 mg for refusal of the medication. She continues to be very withdrawn, guarded, suspicious and paranoid. She is still talking illogically. She is preoccupied with medical issues and somatic concerns. She keeps talking about how Easterseals put her in here because they wanted to experiment on her with medicines. She is still very bizarre and illogical. She sometimes stares into space. The patient has no insight. Patient should participate in more activities and groups. Set firm limits on her." .... K. Brent, M.D.

03/28/03 – "Patient continues to be paranoid, suspicious and delusional. She tends to be argumentative on numerous occasions. She tends to think that there is something wrong with her, and also tends to argue that she was never wrong – meaning her NGRI being in the hospital. She actually showed a letter which she received from Northville Regional Hospital stating she was cleared from NGRI after more than two years of being on NGRI. When I try to discuss that issue she avoids it, and does not want to talk about what happened then. She only wants to talk about the present. Patient has poor insight and is still having a hard time accepting her illness. She is very delusional and bizarre. Continue intensive treatment. She stated that she took the Seroquel last night." .... K. Brent M.D.

03/29/03 – "Patient is still paranoid, delusional and bizarre. After setting firm limits she has been taking the medicines for the last few days. Patient insight into her problems is still poor. She is still delusional and very reclusive." .... K. Brent, M.D.

03/31/2003 – "Patient continues to be paranoid and delusional with psychomotor retardation. She is preoccupied with finding her own psychiatrist. She is rather grandiose. She was informed concerning her need to follow-up with Easterseals Clinic, even if she finds her own psychiatrist. Discharge plans are in process. The social worker is to make arrangements for such plans." .... K. Brent, M.D.

04/01/03 – "Patient continues to be paranoid and suspicious. Discharge plans will be discussed. She wanted to find her own psychiatrist, but she is unable to do so by herself. Therefore, the social worker is to arrange follow-up through Easterseals, where Ms. Ruoss will be receiving her treatment. She is to receive Haldol Decanoate injection tomorrow because of her extensive noncompliance issues." ………. K. Brent, M.D.

04/02/03 – "Patient continues to be paranoid and suspicious. She received a Haldol injection today. She tolerated it well. She has had no dystonia or other side effects. She is doing fairly well and I stressed the importance that she follow-up with Easterseals and the social worker to set up an appointment. Arrangements will be made by the social worker for her to follow-up with Easterseals." ………. K. Brent, M.D.

When I went to court on March 24, 2003, again a court appointed attorney represented me. He was new. I had never had him before. I met with him briefly at the hospital. I was out of this hospital in a little more than two weeks. I received my Discharge Summary and Aftercare Instructions on April 4, 2003 prepared by the psychiatrist/MD. The summary basically talked about "the problem, past psychiatric history, substance abuse history and mental status, recommendations and medications on discharge." My final diagnosis was schizophrenia, paranoid with acute exacerbation; hypertension; arthritis; gastroesophageal reflux disease. Medications to treat this condition are Haldol D 100 mg IM – the next dose was to be given two weeks from April 16, 2003; Seroquel given as 200 mg p.o.q.h.s. It stated that I had medications for my other medical problems.

On the day of my discharge, Ms. Carswell, my Case Manager, drove me home; and, she made follow-up visits to make sure I saw my Easterseals assigned psychiatrist and the nurse for my monthly Haldol injections. This way they were sure I would keep well.

Ms. Carswell remained my Case Manager until she got promoted to a new position. Easterseals assigned me a new Case Manager, Mrs. Mack. I told Mrs. Mack about how my hip stayed sore, and how the skin had gotten hard and rough from the injections. Mrs. Mack was a very sympathetic person. She was not in favor of me having injections. So, she had me put back on Haldol pills. To make sure I took my pills as prescribed, she took me to the pharmacy to get them; and so often came to the apartment to see if I was taking the pills. She even counted how many pills were in the bottle to see if I was up-to-date in taking all the pills. Haldol still wasn't the right med for me, because I would sometimes hear voices very low. But I kept taking the pills as long as Mrs. Mack watched over me. This was Easterseals' concern for me.

Deloris and I were still keeping in touch. As a matter of fact she introduced me to men friends that she knew, just to get me out more. I dated a few of the men she introduced me to, but nothing came out of it. Then she introduced me to Michael. He called and visited me until I stopped answering my phone. (He is discussed later in the book.)

I had begun to call home. (I still call Georgia my home.) I kept in touch with my family now, and I talked to Mom every Sunday. Each time I talked to them, I still believed I was adopted. I stayed depressed because of this; even with Michael visiting and taking me out to dinner at times. I still felt alone.

I made a few trips to Georgia before my mother died in 2006. She was in the hospital for a week, before dying from leg blood clots that moved to her heart. I didn't want to see her ill, so I didn't visit her in the hospital. I went to Georgia a few days after she had passed. I helped my brother and sister arrange the funeral. At the funeral, I could not show any emotions. I have forgiven her, but I will never forget how she had treated me in the past.

When I returned home from Georgia, I decided to start going to a church. I had not been attending church because the Catholic Church was too far away, and I didn't yet have a car. The church I attended, in place of a Catholic Church, was a Baptist Church, since I was a Baptist in the past. The church had its own bus service to transport you there and back home. I met a man who drove the bus. He was a dreamboat. I dated him for a while, and talked to him off and on, until I shut down. Nothing came out of this relationship.

I continued to have services from Easterseals until 2008. I stopped seeing them because I felt that I could make it without them. They wanted me to continue to see their psychiatrist for psychotropic prescriptions and continue to have the services of a Case Worker, but I didn't want to do this. I felt that I was getting along fine, so I even stopped taking my psychotropic meds. I continued taking herbals and supplements. I believed this would take the place of psychotropic meds.

A year passed before I started hearing voice(s) real loud and clear. One thing that stands out in my mind today is that the voice(s) talked about jobs that I should have had and needed to get ready for. I thought what I heard was real, so I believed them. I felt like I could achieve anything. For every job that was mentioned, I made an effort to prepare for it by buying things. Each month, when I got my disability payment, I went to several different types of stores to buy items that would help me on each job. I was told that I would be President, a ballerina, an Olympic swimmer, motorcyclist, beautician, a Ministry of Tourism overseas, and an architect, just to name a few. These were jobs I had never had any experience in, but I believed everything the voices told me. I bought briefcases to use on each job, maps, architect supplies, clothes, a desk top computer, a laptop, GPS system, electronics, three copy machines, telephone systems, cameras...just anything and everything I needed to do each job.

I made a list every month of things to buy. My apartment got so crowded with items I barely had walking room inside. I felt like I was qualified to do anything. I stayed up late at night planning and working with the items I had bought. Sometimes my electric, heat and rent payments were behind because I had spent all my money buying things for jobs. The voice(s) kept me stressed out most of the time because I exerted a lot of effort preparing for these jobs.

In the apartment I continued to experience all kinds of delusion and hallucination happenings. Every other night, I thought I saw a car parked in the lot, facing my living room window, with its lights on. I thought someone was after me, to hurt me. I called the police once or twice. They came out, but couldn't find anything wrong.

In April, 2008, I noticed that my good eye vision was weakening. My sight kept fading from dim to darkness. I saw an ophthalmologist and he immediately had me see a retina specialist. I had a detached retina and needed surgery right away. By having only one good eye, this was devastating news to me. I didn't know how I would manage living not being able to see at all until I healed. I needed someone to be with me during the surgery. I had no family in the area, and Michael and the few people I knew were not close enough as friends for me to call on. Plus, I feared I would be rejected. Deloris was the only person I could ask to help me without fear. She came through again. She was with me when I had the surgery and had me stay with her and her husband Alfred for three months until I was able to see again. I can never forget how they made meals for me, washed my clothes and gave me my eye drops on time. They proved better than a family.

In the early part of 2009, Deloris gave me the news that she and her family were moving down South to live. I felt very disappointed and alone because I had no other close friends, and I did not know what I would do without her being around. When she left I wished her well, but I took it very hard. I started spending more time alone. I isolated myself because I had no other choice, and I did this for a year. I cut myself off from the few people I knew. I didn't even answer my phone when it rang. Michael tried to keep in touch, but I never answered his calls, or returned his calls. Nor did I answer my door for anyone. Once my sister, brother-in-law and brother came from Georgia to visit me. I didn't let them in the apartment. They stayed in a hotel for the night and left for Georgia the next day without seeing me. I still had in my mind that I was an adopted child and they didn't care for me any way. I was holding this against them.

I started to believe the apartment building I lived in was my own. I was obsessed with voice(s) all the time. I was very delusional and hallucinating like before. Once, the voice(s) told me "I had won my stripes in Mecca." When I heard this, I was standing in my living room looking out of the big picture window. The window became a movie screen. I watched a reflection of a scene from the city of Mecca on the window. I saw people walking and fishing in a pond on the glass window pane. It was like sitting in a movie house watching a big screen. It seemed as if I stood there delusional and hallucinating for hours.

The voice(s) also told me not to pay my bills… and I did just that. I continued to spend all of my money on things I really didn't need. I had become a hoarder. I didn't pay my phone or the electric bill. It never occurred to me that the service would be cut off. After all, I thought I owned the complex. Sure enough, the lights got shut off in December, 2009. I had no lights and I couldn't use the stove. I used candles for light. I owned an electric coffee maker and electric frying pan. I had to eat, so I took advantage of the electricity in the apartment Laundry Room, located down the hall from my unit. I used the Laundry Room for cooking. I made coffee and fried foods in the room until I got caught by Management.

The landlord called the police on me. They took me to Southfield Regional Hospital for testing. The Emergency Room Department Staff at the hospital, after examining me and talking to the policemen, documented that, "This is a 61-year old female who is here with possible psych disorder. She is living without electricity or heat. The residents have been complaining because she has been trying to cook with a deep fryer in the common area. All her food is moldy according to the police and it is piled up waist deep in all the rooms and it is clearly spoiled. The police were concerned because the patient was making comments as though she owned the building and then other times more based on reality. Police did call the Adult Protective Services, who recommended that they bring the patient here. The patient denies complaints. She said she is just here for an exam. She does not have any insight into why she is here. She stated, "I don't know why I'm here and that you will have to ask the gentleman. I am here for a checkup." When asked who is the president? I did hear her state to the nurse that she does not keep up with that kind of information. It sounds as though she is somewhat delusional even with the police. Her labs do look normal. Her urine drug screen is negative.

Alcohol is negative. Sugar was a little high at 140. The patient apparently is talking to herself and has a psych history in the past. She did not share that with anyone. We are hydrating her because of her heart rate. I will write a cert on her as she is delusional and she will be transferred to Morrison Hospital psych facility for admission. Diagnosis: Acute psychosis". ...... O. Smith, M.D.

After making these assessments and evaluations the medical staff at Southfield Regional Hospital had me transported by Oakland County EMS to Morrison Hospital in Pontiac.

I was admitted to Morrison Hospital and placed on the Geriatric Psychiatric ward. They gave me an admission evaluation. I had a standard psychiatric examination, a physical examination and routine laboratory blood and urine tests. Test results showed I was blind in my left eye, borderline diabetic mellitus and had high blood pressure in addition to a psychosis. I was placed on a regular diet, but later changed to AHA diet. They started me on Depakene 125 mg, Seroquel 25 mg, Benicar 20 mg, Lisinopril 5 mg and Geodon 10 mg taken every day. I didn't notice any change in how I felt during my entire stay there.

The hospital had daily activities like all the others I had been in. Most times I didn't participate. I just stayed in my room almost all day. I was depressed, but wasn't diagnosed with it until much later. Unlike the other hospitals, though, I was able to select what foods I wanted to eat from a menu they gave me every day. The foods were very well prepared.

There were daily progress notes kept on me. Some of the notes read as follows:

01/01/10 Patient slept on and off tonight. She responds to internal stimuli. Safety maintained. We will continue support and monitoring.

01/02/10 Patient is isolative to her room and still refusing meds. She is cooperative with staff and able to make needs known. We will continue to monitor.

01/04/10 Patient was seen and examined. She denies any complaints. She was sitting on her bed looking through her purse.

01/05/10 Patient's grooming and hygiene are okay. But insight and judgments still are poor. She is still unpredictable. We will continue support and encouragement.

01/06/10 Patient was seen in dining room eating; not verbal. She is still paranoid and suspicious. She was provided support. She refused her Depakene. She slept all through the midnight shift; no problems during safety rounds checks.

01/07/10 Patient is responding to internal stimuli most of the day. She is laughing, talking and smiling with no one around. Her appetite is good, but her affect is paranoid and hallucinating. She refused her meds. Patient was sitting by herself in dining room, and talking to herself. But when confronted, she denied doing so. She refused to go to activities.

01/08/10 Patient is sleeping with lights on at night. She was not redirected to turn the lights off. Patient is still sleeping with her bag full of belongings at her bedside. She is still confused and paranoid. She was provided support. She is agitated, loud and argumentative. She stated that she is "Jesus."

01/11/10 Patient refused her meds. She spit pills into a glass of water. IM was given as ordered.

01/12/10 Patient is seated on her bed with her purse in her lap. She went to court yesterday. We discussed meds and she said she really doesn't need any. She will receive injections if she continues to refuse her meds.

01/15/10 Patient is seated on her bed writing. When I came close to her she covered her pages and said "I don't share my thoughts with anybody." Patient is up ambulating independently on the unit. No inappropriate behavior was observed.

01/16/10 Patient continues to be withdrawn, isolative and her insight and judgment continue to be limited. Provided support and prompting

01/19/10 Patient is in compliance with medications now. She remains in room except for meals. She does not socialize when prompted. Not talking or laughing to herself as much now.

01/20/10 Patient's affect is bright and pleasant. She is cooperative with all unit protocol. Her appetite is good.

01/29/10 Patient is spending a lot of time at my station. She is insisting she is to be discharged today. Although no discharge plans are imminent. Patient is pleasant, cooperative and taking meds. No inappropriate behavior was observed. Social worker contacted Common Ground in order to link patient to Community Mental Health Services. Common Ground indicated that patient has been open at Easterseals, but case has been closed due to noncompliance. Social worker faxed psychosocial information and psych evaluation to Common Ground so patient can be assessed and case reopened.

02/01/10 Social worker met with patient. She has realized her reasons why she has a lot of stuff at home. She is verbal spontaneous and tried to reason out her actions. She is currently complaining to us. Social worker contacted patient's apartment to ensure she can return there. Patient is not evicted per manager and can return to her apartment. But she has no utilities turned on due to nonpayment. Social worker assisted patient in calling Electric Company to have utilities turned back on. Representative asked patient to call back after 5:00 p.m. and pay $406.00 to restore electricity. Patient agreed to do this today. Social Worker will follow-up. And then we will complete discharge planning. Social worker also contacted Adult Protective Services and informed them of her discharge in February, and they agreed to make a home visit in a couple of days to check on the condition of her apartment. Social worker will continue to work on this case. Easterseals is to visit her today to begin Community Mental Health Services. Social worker met Rachel from Easterseals to open up patient's case. Social worker needs to contact Beverly of Easterseals ACT Team to schedule appointment for follow-up care. Patient will require transportation to appointments. Patient is alert, cooperative, pleasant and friendly. No behavioral problems noted.

02/02/10 Social worker met with patient. Patient reported her electricity will be turned on at 5:00 p.m. today. Patient will be discharged at 10:00 a.m. tomorrow departing the hospital by taxi. Social worker called Easterseals to set discharge appointment.

I had spent a little more than a month at Morrison Hospital when I was discharged February 3, 2010. The staff at the hospital contacted Easterseals so that I could resume receiving services from them. I met with Rachel from Easterseals at the hospital before I left. She set up a date for me to return to Easterseals after being discharged.

After having received a number of psychotropic meds at this hospital, I left the hospital with a prescription for Seroquel, and my discharge diagnosis was schizoaffective disorder. I had gone from paranoid schizophrenia to schizoaffective disorder. I had to assure the doctors that I would have the prescription filled, and keep my appointment with Easterseals. Easterseals was there to help me again but I didn't let them.

After I returned home from Morrison Hospital, I didn't do anything the doctor and nurse had asked me to do. I didn't have the prescription filled for Seroquel and I didn't keep my appointment with Easterseals. I was back on my own again. I had no support. My lights were turned on when I got home. The apartment was still cluttered. I didn't make an effort to clear it out because I felt everything in it was something I would eventually use. I had long stopped talking to Deloris (she was out of state), and I wasn't responding to Michael's calls…..nor anyone's' calls. I considered myself as having no friends. I stayed inside mostly and isolated myself. I started to hear voice(s) again. I still thought it was a good sign.

Near the end of 2010 a voice told me "not to pay my rent" because I was going to move to a mansion in Grosse Pointe and I needed the money. I believed the voice and waited for this to happen somehow. I didn't think that I would be evicted from my apartment while I waited. I was blind in my left eye (from the shooting incident in 1995), and now I was blind in my other eye from a cataract. Dr.Monroe, who gave me the retina surgery in 2008, told me at that time that this would possibly happen after the surgery. And that this was one of the side effects. Like my retina, I needed surgery right away for the cataract, but I didn't make a move to have it done, mainly because I didn't have anyone to be with me at the hospital this time.

My vision got so bad it was like looking through waxed paper. This got worse and worse. My electric was shut off again because

I was spending all my money buying items the voice(s) told me to buy. An eviction notice was placed on my door. I ignored it and didn't believe this was happening to me. In October, 2010 I was evicted from this apartment. In his petition, my landlord's reasons for evicting me were, "Electric is shut off, cooking in common areas which is a fire hazard, and refusal to stop on several occasions." Being behind in rent payments wasn't an issue for my eviction.

I ignored the Eviction Notice on my door, and I didn't show up in court. On the day of the eviction, I mentioned to the landlord that I was blind (My doctor had diagnosed me as being legally blind in my good eye). I had hoped that he would at least let me stay there until I could see well enough to leave. Instead, he gave me one week to move my furniture and belongings. This was impossible for me to do because I had no one to help me move, nor did I have the money to move. He called the police that day. They knew that I had a mental health problem right away. It could have been because my behavior wasn't normal or from my past police record. I still don't know to this day. The police took me to Common Ground for Screening and Evaluation. Common Ground did an assessment and had me admitted to Mt Pleasant General Hospital (psychiatric ward).

The assessment came out to be quite similar to all the other evaluations I had before. The examiner stated that, "I was schizophrenic paranoid type. Patient is acutely psychotic responding to internal stimuli, talking to herself and laughing inappropriately. She admits to hearing voices of God and angels. She stated that she was evicted from her apartment. Patient has paranoid delusion and she has a history of violence in the past. Therefore, there is a likelihood of injury to others. She does not understand the need for treatment. She states that she has no mental problems and refuses treatment. Hospitalization is recommended for her." ……….. Scott Perriman Psychiatrist

I was petitioned under court order to be admitted to Mt Pleasant General Hospital the end of October 2010. I contacted the landlord of my apartment and informed him I was in the hospital. He still gave me one week to move my belongings out of the apartment. I had no way of doing this, so while in the hospital I lost everything I

owned…furniture, pictures, books, clothes, electronics, plants, etc…
everything in the apartment. The only thing I had left were the
clothes I was wearing and a bag of jewelry I walked out with.

This hospital was not much different from the others I had been
in….except for a few things. Every morning before breakfast we were
weighed. There were activities every day and progress notes kept by
a clinician. The patients never went outside of the hospital's doors. I
stayed indoors during my entire stay there. Every day I had my vitals
checked, and, on some days the nurse or psychiatrist would ask me
how I felt. What I do remember is that I stayed in bed a lot, and they
let me. I didn't want to be bothered with anyone as always. I kept to
myself as usual. I didn't know I was depressed, until diagnosed later
while being in this hospital. Some of the progress notes kept on me
read as follows:

10/26/10 Patient is still acting according to her petition. She states that
she has no mental illness and refuses treatment. On admission,
patient was calm and cooperative; she denied having suicidal
homicidal ideation regardless of her past history. Patient is placed
on Level III and settled in her room. Patient is legally blind and
has been placed on falls precautions. She wears a prosthetic in
her left eye. Patient affect is angry; she is very unhappy over
her eviction and states, "I don't know who they think they are."
Patient makes no eye contact. Patient called her family to come
to get her stuff, but they couldn't because of their own problems.
Patient is homeless.

10/27/10 Patient was resting in bed at start of shift. Patient got
up for meals. She was walking to dining room talking to self.
Patient does admit to hearing voices; her affect is angry. She did
not admit to any other symptoms. Her appetite is good. We will
continue to monitor mood and behavior.

10/28/10 Patient said, "I sometimes hear voices, but I don't pay
attention to them". Patient denies any suicidal thoughts, and
depression. Patient says, "I am here because they claimed I was
cooking in the hallway." Patient denies any type of hallucinations

at the current time. Patient complained of pain in the lower back. She was given Tylenol. She consumed breakfast and lunch. She has good hygiene; not body odor. Her affect is sad; some eye contact. Patient has attended group gathering. Patient not aware of reason she is here.

10/29/10 Patient observed talking to herself quite regularly. She recognizes she is talking to herself. Patient denies having any pain today. Patient attended exercise group with some participation. She has minimal interaction with others. She is responsive when prompted. She had poor eye contact. Patient is visible in the unit, but returns to bed quite often. Patient is compliance with medications. She attends group therapy.

10/30/10 Patient states that her mind is too busy thinking and making plans for real estate. She says, "I am gonna be back in it"- "just trying to straighten things out." She is still isolative, but visible. Patient observed responding to internal stimuli. Eye contact poor; does not interact with peers. Patient denies depression, but has disheveled look and shows altered thinking process.

10/31/10 Patient asked "where is my food, because I am hungry." Patient denies depression; eye contact poor; affect flat. Does not interact with peers; did not attend groups. Alter thought process and responding to internal stimuli. Patient is talking out loud to self. Offered supported approach and positive reinforcement.

11/02/10 Patient's mood is stable; affect bright, pleasant. She is still responding to internal stimuli, but less than a day ago. Thought process still altered. Responses and thoughts are sometimes logical too. Patient knows about her housing needs. Patient is making phone calls to help assist in finding a place to live. We will continue to monitor patient's behavior for safety. Encouraged patient to verbalize feelings and concerns. Offered supportive approach.

11/10/10 Used supportive approach and encouraged patient to attend more groups. She is concerned about her living arrangements when she is discharged. She is in bed sick with a cold.

11/11/10 Dr.Boffer was called and gave patient Claritin.

11/13/10 Patient is feeling better, but stays under covers. The heater doesn't work in her room. Patient's mood is pleasant. She interacts with roommate but that is about all. Eye contact is fair. Patient denies depression; but has some anxiety. Patient has very little insight. She is very isolative. Will continue to monitor mood and encourage her to attend groups to educate herself on her illness. Patient says "yes the voice is still there." Patient says, "I ask a question and I always get a response." She became angry when suggested that perhaps this was not a voice, but her own thoughts. She said, "I know my own thoughts."

11/15/10 Patient continues to deny having any psychiatric symptoms. Patient was visible on the unit for dinner after being prompted by staff. Patient was pleasant during interaction with staff, but did not interact with peers. Patient was not observed responding to internal stimuli.

Her mood is isolative, and her affect mixed.

11/22/10 Patient states, "I'm okay and I don't want to hurt myself or no one else." Patient states, "I'm just waiting for them to find me a place to live." Patient is up and down and visible on unit. When patient is up, she dresses. Patient hygiene is fine. Appetite is good. Patient observed having a little social interaction on unit. Patient also observed in her bedroom. Her mood is guarded; off and on isolated; no motivation. She is pleasant to others. Her thought process is focused on a place to live. Patient denies responding to internal stimuli. She is compliance with medications and lab testing on the unit. She is showing progress toward her treatment plan.

11/23/10 Patient is isolated in her room. She has poor peer interactions. Patient affect is pleasant. Patient denies all psychotic symptoms. Encouraged patient to verbalize feelings and concerns, and to interact with peers and attend group activities.

11/24/10 Patient is cooperative. She is eating 100% of meals. She attends groups. Denies auditory hallucinations. Flat affect at times. Encouraged verbalization of feelings and to interact more with peers.

During this hospitalization, I developed a talent for writing. My thinking had reached a point where I was writing poems and coming up with pages of my own poetry. I also drew architectural layouts, which I had never learned to do before. In my mind, I felt that I could do this. I couldn't see very well, because of the cataract, so I had to write with a black magic marker, which the nurse gave me. My words were written in extra-large letters. I used anything to write on – paper which I got from the desk, or even the napkins I didn't use at meal time. All I wanted to do was to write and draw. I felt I could do something with my ideas after being released from the hospital, so I kept my material in my bedside drawer, and I brought everything with me when I was released.

Dr. Long, my doctor, placed me on Desyrel, Lopressor, Trazodone, Risperidal and Venlafaxine. I took the Lopressor for high blood pressure. They made sure I took these meds twice a day, every day. He diagnosed me as having paranoid schizophrenia, chronic, with acute exacerbation, major depression, hypertension and legal blindness secondary to cataract in right eye, and trauma to the left eye. I had been depressed for years, but none of the other psychiatrists had recognized it. I stayed in Mt Pleasant General Hospital a little more than a month before being released November 28, 2010. My discharge summary read as follows:

"Ms. Ruoss, a 61-year old African-American female, was admitted to Mt Pleasant General Hospital inpatient mental health unit on October 25, 2010. She was admitted because of acute increased self-harm and other harm risk. The patient was increasingly noncompliant with her medications and increasingly psychotic burning food in the laundry room of her apartment and not being able to take care of her personal hygiene and other affairs. She has been noncompliant with her Easterseals' outpatient care. Because of her increasingly bizarre behavior, responses to internal stimuli, it was felt she be hospitalized for her protection. She is legally blind but can see out of her right eye, which does have a cataract in it. She was able to ambulate about the unit when she chose to, quite rapidly. Initial mental status was that of an elderly African-American female wandering by the desk. She was playing with the telephone in my room when I left her alone for a few moments. Her mood and affect were hypomanic. Speech was clear, rapid and laughing. She had paranoid delusions, hearing voices. The voices were telling her that she was a failure and states that she has $2 million of jewelry in a hospital lockup. She was oriented to time, place, and person. Memory was selective. Insight was poor, judgment poor. Intellectual activity was average. It was felt she was suffering from paranoid schizophrenia, chronic with acute exacerbation. The presence of major depression was also considered, or hypomania. A physical assessment was performed also by Dr. Boffer. The assessment was reflective of hypertension along with the problems with her eyes. She also had an assessment for her eyes. It was suggested that she have outpatient care and treatment for the cataract following discharge. The patient did have some laboratory studies performed as part of her evaluation; which came out essentially normal. The patient from a psychiatric standpoint was treated with individual and group psychotherapy, recreational and occupational therapy and medication. She was placed on antipsychotic Risperdal an antidepressant medication. However, she seemed to respond very poorly to this and remained almost attached to her bed, very seldom getting out of bed. As a result, she was placed on Abilify. However, this did not prove to be effective. In fact, it was less effective than the Risperdal, so the patient was transferred back to the Risperdal, which had been more effective and then was more effective definitely in reducing her psychotic symptoms and a lot of hallucinations and delusions. The patient slowly began to improve over the week prior to discharge, and at the time of discharge, November 28, 2010, she was taking the following medications on that being Risperdal 2 mg twice a day, Effexor 75 mg twice a day, Desyrel 50 mg h.s., and Lopressor 25 mg daily. There were no complications noted during the hospitalization and at the time of discharge. My final diagnosis at the time of discharge was: Paranoid schizophrenia, chronic with acute exacerbation; major depression; hypertension and legal blindness secondary to cataract in right eye and trauma to the left eye. We have made arrangements for the patient to reside in an adult foster care home." .... Dr. G. Long, Psychiatrist

The hospital supplied me with enough medication for thirty days after I was discharged. For the first time I was taking medications with no side effects.

When I was released, I would have stayed homeless if it wasn't for a Social Worker at the hospital. She knew I had no home to go to. So she found me an Adult Foster Care Home to live in, in Southfield, MI. Mrs. Camilla, the owner of the home, came to the hospital the week of Thanksgiving to interview me. I moved to her home that same week. God was on my side. Mrs. Camilla was a blessing.

When I came to her home, my eyesight had gotten worse. I had to be led around because of my blindness. Mrs. Camilla took me to a surgeon who gave me the cataract surgery. Even though I have one good eye, I see very well now, thanks to Mrs. Camilla's concern and speedy follow-up.

Living in a group home was nothing new to me because I had lived at the R & K Home after my discharge from the hospital in 2000. Like before, there were rules and chores, and having to go to a day program. I wasn't hearing the voices as much now, but I did sleep a lot. I was still somewhat depressed and kept very quiet and to myself. I didn't hesitate taking my meds when the caregiver at the home passed out meds morning and at bedtime. Easterseals did their follow-up, also. I am certain that with all I encountered with the cataract condition, would not had happen had I been using Easterseals' services at the time. They would have taken me for the cataract surgery as soon as they found out I needed it.

Estella Green, from Easterseals, was assigned to the home I lived in. She became my Case Manager and made a visit to see me at least once a week. Estella made sure I was satisfied with my new home, kept watch on my prescriptions, and took me to doctor appointments, just like the others. Easterseals was back in my life again, and I don't regret it. I made an effort to overcome my depression and my medicines were helping. I was now on Risperidone, Venlafaxine and Trazodone once a day.

I tried to stay awake and make conversation with people at the home. Within two years, the combination of the medicine, my personal efforts and my prayers were working. I wasn't hearing voices now and I wasn't depressed. I proved to be helpful, friendly and trustworthy at the home. I wasn't hard to live with and I was more "high functioning" than my housemates. Therefore, Mrs. Camilla gave me more privileges than the others.

I started to call people I knew in the past, people that I thought would reject me before. I made contact with Michael, and much to my surprise, he was glad to hear from me. I didn't hold back from him what I had gone through. I told him all about the hospitals, group homes...everything. He showed no stigma against me. Regardless of my illness, he wanted to see me. We had lunch together, and as of today, we are still seeing each other. Mrs. Camilla even let me spend weekends at his house whenever I wanted to, just as long as she knew where I would be, and I got back home at a certain time.

I started getting out more. I joined a gym, and she allowed me to go to a day program on days I didn't go to the gym. She wanted me to be occupied every day and not in bed sleeping and I *wanted* to keep busy. Even though I pretty much ran my own show at the group home, I still wanted to have my own apartment. Mrs. Camilla didn't object to my wanting to leave.

Part VII

GETTING BETTER

Mrs. Green and my psychiatrist were very concerned about me. I had started to open up to people, and they listened to what I had to say. I wanted to move, to be independent again and I felt I could handle it. Easterseals thought so, too. Mrs. Green helped me find a place of my own. Easterseals, for the second time, helped me get set up in an apartment in March, 2014. I did have some fears about starting over again and being on my own. This is normal...I'm told.

I am still seeing a psychiatrist at Easterseals, but only every two months now. That's how much better I am. I have also gone through group therapy at Easterseals. These sessions taught me so much about mental illness just through interacting with my peers. I now have an independent therapist, who I see every two weeks. Eleanor, my therapist, and I talk about everything. She helps me to understand my life better.

It's been a long journey having been on different psychotropic meds and having been in seven different hospitals. After being treated at Mt Pleasant General Hospital and seeing an Easterseals psychiatrist, I can say I feel better than I have ever felt in my life. I feel like a new person. Being on meds that work for me has helped me to see just how out of touch with reality I had been in the past.

Now I make an effort not to isolate myself from others and I try to keep busy. I take my meds every day, and on time. I'm now sociable and outgoing. I do regulate my activities, so as not to become too stressed. Somedays I go through a mild depression wanting to just stay in bed. This is a sign of getting depressed, my therapist told me, and that it is quite normal for one who has had a chronic depression before as I have had. In order to combat this, Eleanor said, "plan to get up a certain time every morning. This will eventually go away." I have done this, and I plan each day of my life.

I also have a Wellness Toolbox that I can go to when necessary. I learned about this in a (WRAP), Wellness Recovery Action Plan for Trauma Class, I attended at Easterseals. The Wellness Toolbox contains items that will comfort me when I am depressed. I haven't had to use it yet. Every day I have something to do. I try to go to the gym two to three times a week. I attend Michael's Catholic Church with him on Sundays. I spend time sewing, reading, crocheting and entering sweepstakes as a hobby when I'm home. I keep my real estate license active by attending continuing education classes. I am also busy being a notary public. I also listen to soothing music and cook new foods when I feel creative.

I have made more friends than I have ever had, and they keep in touch. Better yet, I respond to them. I attend Easterseals Dreams Unlimited Clubhouse, a psychosocial rehabilitation program. Easterseals Dreams Unlimited Clubhouse is a place where I go when I don't want to be home alone. I have made quite a few friends there. We all have something in common – mental illness. We offer support to each other. I'm able to talk to my peers about their illnesses and meds, listen to their stories, and they listen to mine. All of us keep busy running the Clubhouse with the help of staff. We have tasks of our choice to do each day. Tasks may include handling money, doing clerical jobs, cooking or household jobs. At Easterseals

Dreams Unlimited Clubhouse, I am able to keep up my computer and administrative skills.

When I have free time, I go to Daisies 4 U Adult Day Center, a day program where I am into arts, crafts and crocheting. This keeps me relaxed. I also attend a Women's Group Therapy session at Easterseals on Fridays. Here a group of women talk and share their concerns on any issue. I feel relieved after attending these sessions.

I am a member of three committees and two workgroups through OCHN (Oakland Community Health Network). Each group meets once a month and sometimes more. It is a blessing for me to be able to advocate for and support other mentally challenged persons by being on these committees and workgroups. When there are other events and affairs sponsored by OCHN or its providers, I am present. I have attended many classes, rallies and conferences sponsored by these organizations. I assisted in planning the first Your Voice, Your Value Annual Conference hosted by OCHN in 2016. I was awarded the 2017 Dan Moran Award given each year by OCHN, and in 2018 I was selected, along with another person, to carry the flag representing Oakland County Community Mental Health in a Walk-A-Mile In My Shoes rally held every year at the Capitol in Lansing, Michigan.

I found time to help out Michael with his mother before she passed with dementia two years ago. I have made and still have many friends, both women and men, whom I keep in contact with. All in all, I can say, I am enjoying my new life. Michael is very much in my life now; and if it wasn't for him, I don't know what I would do. He is a great support and has helped in my recovery. Michael brought hope, joy, comfort and encouragement to my life. He doesn't look at me as if I am ill. He sees me as a human being….his girl. He has accepted my illness. He's there when I need him, and he would have been there to help me in the past when I really needed help, if only I had contacted him. He loves me just that much. Here is what he has to say:

"Initially after meeting Betty, I became aware of issues which plagued her. These issues eventually culminated in eviction, hospitalization, and eventual recovery. However, I was fortunate enough to be a part of, and witness to, this most remarkable recovery and transformation into the person that Betty is now. Yet guilt feelings remain for me, regarding the help I was unable to give Betty during the times she struggled mentally. I firmly believe that my personal circumstances, including caring for a mother with advanced dementia during these past years, actually played a positive role in Betty's recovery.

Having Mom and I to care for and assist, I believe, actually helped Betty as she became a strong leader, displaying her solid organizational and planning skills while caring for myself and my family. Also, having to take time to care for herself helped Betty.

Betty's recovery is nothing short of remarkable. Today her weekly schedule rivals a thirty-year old...numerous committees, group activities and special projects fill her time. Many friends and telephone calls from them take up more of her time as well.

Betty's recovery is amazing and complete, making a 360° turnaround. Today, she is one of the most intelligent, personable and confident persons that I know." ....*Michael*

If you are reading this book and suffer from a mental illness, or even if you support someone with a mental illness, I'd like to offer this advice:

1 Mental illness can be treated just like any other disease. Medication is getting better and better and more specific now. Always take your medication(s). If it does not agree with you and you do have side effects, tell your doctor about this, so that he/she can change med(s) or make an adjustment. This is where I made my mistake; I didn't speak up until much later in my illness. Remember, medications can take time to work and provide symptom relief. You and your doctor may

have to try a few different options to find the medication(s) that manages your symptoms and works best for you. People with schizophrenia who stop taking their medication are 5 times more likely to relapse than those who continue to take their medication. Think about the benefits of taking your med(s), and then you are more apt to take it. In addition to med(s), some supportive treatments that can be a part of your recovery include: Going to therapy; Attending support groups; Finding safe and stable housing; Training in daily living and social skills; and, Staying active (going to the gym, out for a walk, or to the library).

2   Avoid gaps in care. It is said, "People with a mental illness die twenty-five years earlier than people without a mental illness." If this is the case, it is wise to take care of other health issues you might have as well. People who experience gaps in care are more likely to have relapses, end up back in the hospital and have a reduced quality of life. This happened to me. After leaving the hospital, you want to make sure you stay well. Think positive, stay busy, be patient and take one step at a time. One way to avoid setbacks is to use the outpatient services provided for you in your community. When you are in the hospital, usually a treatment team member will set up outpatient or community-based services for you before you are discharged. Be sure to follow-up. In your recovery journey, there will be ups and downs. You have good times when you manage your symptoms and you feel strong and in control. And there are hard times, when symptoms worsen and your recovery is interrupted. The good news is there are strategies to help you stay on track. You can play an important role by being aware of triggers and symptoms, managing your stress, taking medication regularly, and by having a crisis plan.

3   Here are some helpful ways to remember to take your medications: Take your meds at the same time every day. By doing this, it becomes a habit. Use a pillbox or calendar labeled

with the days of the week; tape a note to your television or channel changer. I usually write "Take your meds" on a 3x5" paper with a black marker and place it where I can see it; you can also tape a reminder to the mirror in your bathroom or on the refrigerator; use your cell phone's calendar reminder; have a friend or family member call to remind you or leave your medication out where you can see it.

4   It is important to set goals. Recovery is hard work but it can be done. Setting goals and achieving them can help you live the life you want while managing your mental health recovery. Set goals that are important to you; what you want to accomplish and what you want out of life. Some examples might be taking classes; making your current living or housing situation better; renewing a personal relationship. It is best to start with short-term goals rather than long-term goals that may take months or even years to accomplish. Talk to someone about your goals. This can help you realize how far you've come, so you can better deal with any challenges you are facing. Having hope and thinking positively can help you deal with challenges and inspire you to achieve your goals.

Last, but not least, is the issue of stigma. Stigma has been around for a long time, although, society has become more accepting and understanding of mental health issues in recent years. You may have been made to feel disrespected, excluded, embarrassed, inadequate, sad or scared. Or you may have been labeled as stupid and unworthy. This stigma causes people to feel ashamed and prevents many from seeking the help they need and speaking out about their mental illness. To cope with the stigma of mental illness, people with mental illness and their families can take certain steps to help such as:

1   Keep hope and remember that treatment works. Many individuals with mental illness enjoy productive lives. I am living proof of this. Safe and effective medications and

psychotherapy are available, and newer treatments are being developed every day.

2 Praise your loved one for seeking help. People need to be patient in trying new medications, coping with side effects, and learning new behaviors. Helping your loved one to feel good about him or herself is important.

3 Remain active. Social isolation can be a negative side effect of the stigma linked to mental illness. Isolation can put you at a high risk for depression. I had to learn not to isolate myself.

4 Surround yourself with supportive people. Ceasing to participate in activities you or your loved one enjoy puts you at high risk for depression and burnout. Take a risk and try new activities in your community.

5 Remember that you are not alone. Many people cope with similar situations. People commonly struggle with schizophrenia, depression, anxiety, substance abuse and other mental illnesses.

Remember that mental illness is nothing to be ashamed of, but the "stigma and bias shame us all." .... Bill Clinton.

God Bless and Best of Luck!

CELEBRITIES AND FAMOUS
PEOPLE WITH MENTAL ILLNESS

Abraham Lincoln	-	**Depression**
Alexander Hamilton	-	**Depression**
Alexander Graham Bell	-	**Dyslexia**
Alexander the Great	-	**Depression**
Andrew Jackson	-	**Depression**
Andy Goram	-	**Schizophrenia**
Aretha Franklin	-	**Panic Anxiety Disorder**
Axel Rose	-	**Bipolar**
Barbara Bush	-	**Depression, Anxiety**
Beatrice Arthur	-	**Depression**
Betty Ford	-	**Depression**
Bobby Darin	-	**Depression**
Calvin Coolidge	-	**Depression**
Carley Simon	-	**Social Phobia, Panic Disorder**
Charles 'Buddy' Bolden	-	**Schizophrenia**
Charles Faust	-	**Schizophrenia**
Charles Schultz	-	**Anxiety**
Courtney Love	-	**Depression**
Daniel Boorstin	-	**Bipolar**
Danny Kaye	-	**Depression**
Drew Carey	-	**Depression**
Eddie Fisher	-	**Depression**

Ellen DeGeneres	-	**Depression**
Eric Clapton	-	**Depression**
Florence Nightingale	-	**Depression**
Francis Ford Coppola	-	**Bipolar**
Hans Christian Anderson	-	**Bipolar**
Howie Mandel	-	**OCD**
James Farmer	-	**Depression**
James Garner	-	**Depression**
James Joyce	-	**Panic Disorder**
Jeff Conaway	-	**Depression**
Jim Carrey	-	**Depression**
John Denver	-	**Depression**
John Nash	-	**Schizophrenia**
Johnny Depp	-	**Anxiety Disorder**
Jose Cansero	-	**Depression**
JP Morgan	-	**Depression**
Judy Garland	-	**Depression**
Kenneth Branagh	-	**Depression**
King David	-	**Depression**
King George III	-	**Depression**
Leonard Bernstein	-	**Depression**
Lionel Adridge	-	**Schizophrenia**
Louie Anderson	-	**Depression**
Ludwig Van Beethoven	-	**Bipolar**
Lyndon Baines Johnson	-	**Depression**
Marilyn Monroe	-	**Depression**
Marlon Brando	-	**Depression**
Martin Luther	-	**Depression**
Mel Gibson	-	**Depression**
Menachem Begin	-	**Depression**
Naomi Campbell	-	**Anxiety Disorder**
Naomi Judd	-	**Panic Disorder**
Napoleon Bonaparte	-	**Depression**

"PEOPLE WITH MENTAL ILLNESS ENRICH OUR LIVES."

Ned Beatty	-	**Bipolar**
Nicholas Cage	-	**Anxiety Disorder**
Noel Coward	-	**Depression**
Oprah Winfrey	-	**Anxiety Disorder, Depression**
Phil Graham	-	**Depression**
Queen Elizabeth	-	**Depression**
Richard Dreyfuss	-	**Depression**
Richard Simmons	-	**Anorexia, Bulimia**
Robert Downey, Jr.	-	**Bipolar**
Ron Ellis	-	**Depression**
Rona Barrett	-	**Depression**
Roseanne Barr	-	**Depression, Agoraphobia, Depression**
Sally Field	-	**Anxiety Disorder**
Samuel Becket	-	**Depression**
Shecky Greene	-	**Bipolar, Panic Disorder**
Syd Barrett	-	**Schizophrenia, Depression**
Theodore Roosevelt	-	**Bipolar**
Thomas Edison	-	**Depression**
Tracy Gold	-	**Anorexia**
Ty Cobb	-	**Depression**
Vaslov Nijnsky	-	**Schizophrenia**
Victor Hugo	-	**Depression**
Vincent Van Gogh	-	**Bipolar**
Virginia Woolf	-	**Bipolar**
Willard Scott	-	**Panic Disorder**
Winston Churchill	-	**Bipolar**

"PEOPLE WITH MENTAL ILLNESS ENRICH OUR LIVES."

Glossary of Terms

<u>ACT (TEAM)</u> - Assertive Community Treatment – a multidisciplinary clinical team approach of providing 24 hour, intensive community services in the individual's natural setting (i.e., home community).

<u>AGORAPHOBIA</u> – An abnormal and persistent fear of public places or open areas, especially those from which escape could be difficult or in which help might not be immediately accessible. Persons with agoraphobia frequently also have panic disorder.

<u>ALCOHOLISM</u> – A disease that can be arrested but not cured. One of the symptoms is an uncontrollable desire to drink. Alcoholism is a progressive illness. As long as alcoholics continue to drink, their drive to drink will get worse. If not dealt with, the disease can result in insanity or death.

<u>ALTERATION OF THE SENSES</u> - The senses (sight, hearing, touch, and/or smell) may be intensified and/or distorted, especially early in schizophrenia.

<u>ANOREXIA BULIMIA</u> – An eating disorder characterized by an abnormally low body weight, intense fear of gaining weight and a distorted perception of body weight. People with anorexia place a high value on controlling their weight and shape. To prevent weight gain or to continue losing weight, people with anorexia bulimia usually severely restrict the amount of food they eat. They control calorie intake by vomiting after eating or by misusing laxatives, diet aids, and diuretics of enemas.

ANTIANXIETY AGENT - Medication used to reduce anxiety, relax muscles and produce sedation.

ANTIDEPRESSANT MEDICATION - Medication used to treat severe depression.

ANTIPSYCHOTIC MEDICATION - Medication used for treatment of the symptoms of psychosis, which include unusual or bizarre behavior, hallucinations, delusion, agitation, and disturbed thought processes.

BIPOLAR – A mental illness that typically includes extreme shifts in mood, energy, and functioning that include mania and depression.

BULIMIA NERVOSA – An eating disorder characterized by binge eating followed by purging. The person has regular episode of overeating and feels a loss of control. The person then uses different ways such as vomiting or laxatives (purging), to prevent weight gain.

CASE MANAGER - A trained professional working with people who have a mental illness and who helps a person obtain services and supports that are goal oriented and individualized.

CHANGES IN BEHAVIOR - (A sign and symptom of schizophrenia.) Slowness of movement, inactivity, and withdrawing are common. Motor abnormalities such as grimacing, posturing, odd mannerisms, or ritualistic behavior are sometimes present. There may also be pacing, rocking, or apathetic immobility.

CHANGES IN EMOTIONS - (A sign and symptom of schizophrenia.) Early in the illness, the person may feel widely varying, rapidly fluctuating emotions and exaggerated feelings, particularly guilt and fear. Emotions are often inappropriate to the situation. Later there may be apathy, lack of drive, and loss of interest and ability to enjoy activities.

COMMON GROUND SANCTUARY RESOURCE & CRISIS CENTER, Oakland County Michigan - Common Ground provides a lifeline for individuals and families in Oakland County who are in crisis, victims of crime, persons with mental illness, people trying to cope with critical situations and runaway and homeless youths. Helping people in need for more than 40 years, Common Ground serves more than 80,000 individuals per year.

CULTURE SHOCK - An experience a person may have when one moves to a cultural environment which is different from one's own; it is also the life due to immigration or a visit to a new country, or a move between social environments.

DAISIES 4 U ADULT DAY CENTER - Provides opportunities for adult clients to come together in settings and atmospheres of eminence and superiority as a group, for services and activities which support their independence while encouraging their involvement in the day program and the surrounding communities. Also, to enhance the lives of the aging and challenged population by providing trust, respect, therapeutic service, education, socialization, entertainment, and life transitional skills in a safe and wholesome environment.

DAN MORAN AWARD - Presented yearly by OCHN. The individual who receives the Dan Moran Award actively promotes the rights of individuals, encourages self-advocacy, raises awareness about developmental disabilities, mental illness, and substance use disorder; breaks down boundaries, and serves as a role model to others. Dan Moran was a passionate advocate for persons with disabilities. As an OCHN Recipients Rights trainer, he instilled hope and demonstrated that dreams are possible for all people.

DELUSIONS – Delusions are basically false ideas that the person believes to be true, but which cannot be, and to which the individual firmly adheres despite well-reasoned arguments.

Paranoid Delusions -- characterized by belief that one is being watched, controlled, or persecuted. Grandiose Delusions -- centered on the belief that one owns wealth or has special power, or is a famous person, often political or religious. Delusions are the result of over acuteness or disruptions of the senses and an inability to synthesize and respond appropriately to stimuli. To the person experiencing them, they are real.

DEPRESSION - Loss of interest in once pleasurable activities coming out of nowhere, unrelated to events or circumstances; expressions of hopelessness; excessive fatigue and sleepiness; inability to sleep, pessimism; perceiving the world as "dead"; thinking or talking about suicide.

DYSLEXIA – Characterized by trouble with reading despite normal intelligence. Different people are affected to varying degrees. Problems may include difficulties in spelling words, reading quickly, writing words, "sounding out" words in the head, pronouncing words when reading aloud and understanding what one reads.

EASTERSEALS DREAMS UNLIMITED CLUBHOUSE - Accredited by Clubhouse International, Easterseals Dreams Unlimited is a psychosocial rehabilitation program. It is a member-driven program that exists to instill a sense of belonging, provide support, and increase independence for persons diagnosed with serious mental illness. Members join the Clubhouse for various reasons and each brings with them a unique package of talents, skills and goals. It is the purpose of the Clubhouse to provide a place where those talents and skills can be utilized, thus helping members achieve their personal as well as Clubhouse goals within a very friendly and supported environment.

EASTERSEALS MICHIGAN - Easterseals Michigan serves and supports people with disabilities or special needs and their families so they can successfully live, learn, work and play in their communities. Easterseals' mission is to create solutions that change lives of children and adults with disabilities or other special needs and their families.

GROUP HOME - A group home is a private residence, for children or young people who cannot live with their families, or people with chronic disabilities who may be adults or seniors. It may be a small supervised residential facility, as for mentally ill people or wards of the state in which residents typically participate in daily tasks and are often free to come and go on a voluntary basis. It is a substitute home usually located in a residential neighborhood. Typically there are no more than six residents and there is at least one trained caregiver there 24 hours a day.

HALLUCINATIONS - Hallucinations are sensory perceptions with no external stimuli. The most common hallucinations are auditory; hearing "voices" which the person may be unable to distinguish from the voices of real people. Hallucinations are the result of over acuteness or disruptions of the senses and an inability to synthesize and respond appropriately to stimuli. To the person experiencing them, they are real.

HYPOMANIA – A condition similar to mania but less severe. The symptoms are similar with elevated mood, increase activity, decreased need for sleep, grandiosity, racing thoughts and the like.

INABILITY TO PROCESS INFORMATION AND RESPOND APPROPRIATELY - (Also known as "thought disorder") Because individuals with schizophrenia have difficulty processing external sights and sounds, and because they experience internal stimuli that others are not aware of; their responses are often illogical or inappropriate. Their thought patterns are characterized by faulty logic, disorganized or incoherent speech, blocking, and sometimes neologisms (made-up-words). They may relate experiences and concepts in a way that seems illogical to others, but that holds great meaning and significance for themselves.

JOB CORPS – A program administered by the United States Department of Labor that offers free-of-charge education and vocational training to young men and women ages 16 to 24.

KEVIN'S LAW - The purpose of Kevin's Law is to enable the court to order "Assisted Outpatient Treatment" for people with a mental illness who are the "least able to help themselves or most likely to present a risk to others."

KKK – (The Ku Klux Klan-(1865) – The Ku Klux Klan (KKK) is organized in Pulaski, Tennessee. The KKK terrorizes and intimidates African Americans and their white allies through countless assaults, lynchings and fire-bombings.

MANIA – A mood disorder in which people feel incredibly excited, hyperactive, and overly optimistic. Mania is also one part of bipolar disorder also known as manic depression in which people swing from being depressed to being manic (being in a state of mania). Often times people who are manic enjoy the state and get a sense of pleasure from it since during the state they are so optimistic and energetic.

MENTAL ILLNESS - A medical condition disrupting a person's thinking, feeling, mood, ability to relate to others, and daily functioning. One in four people will develop a mental illness in their lifetime. Most mental illnesses can be treated effectively with medication, therapy, diet, exercise, and support. Recovery is possible.

MILD DEPRESSION - Dysthymia (recurring, mild depression) Dysthymia is a type of chronic, milder depression. More days than not, you feel mildly or moderately depressed, although you may have brief periods of normal mood. The symptoms of dysthymia are not as strong as the symptoms of major depression, but they last much longer. Some people also experience major depressive episodes on top of dysthymia, a condition known as "double depression". If you suffer from dysthymia, you may feel like you have always suffered from depression. Or you may think that your continuous depressed state is just "normal". However, dysthymia can be treated, even if your symptoms of depression have gone untreated for years.

MOOD DISORDER - The term mood refers to the state of one's emotions. A mood disorder is marked by periods of extreme sadness (depression) or excitement (mania) or both. Some hypomania symptoms are: Decreased need to sleep, short temper, argumentativeness, delusional thinking, boundless energy and activities which have painful consequences such as spending sprees or reckless driving.

MY PLACE - CENTER FOR WELLNESS - (Formerly "South Oakland Drop-In-Center") My Place Center for Wellness, located in Oakland County, Michigan, provides a warm and caring environment where adults at any stage in the mental health recovery process can engage in casual social and recreational activities with other adults. Individuals have the opportunity to learn about themselves and others while they work on their self-directed recovery plans with support and encouragement from the My Place staff.

NAACP – (National Association for the Advancement of Colored People) – A civil rights organization in the United States, formed in 1909 as a bi-racial organization to advance justice for African Americans. Its mission in the 21st century is to "ensure the political, educational, social and economic equality of rights of all persons and to eliminate racial hatred and racial discrimination.

OCHN - (Oakland Community Health Network) - The public mental health system responsible for identifying, influencing, and delivering services and supports to approximately 26,000 Oakland County residents, including individuals with intellectual/developmental disabilities, adults with mental illness, children with serious emotional disturbance, and persons with substance use disorders.

OCD - (Obsessive Compulsive Disorder) Obsessions are repeated, intrusive, unwanted thoughts that cause extreme anxiety. Compulsions are ritual behaviors that a person uses to diminish anxiety. People with OCD feel the need to check things repeatedly, or have certain thoughts or perform routines and rituals over and over. Examples are hand washing, counting, repeated checking, and repeating a word or action.

PANIC DISORDER - People with panic disorder have sudden and repeated attacks of fear that last for several minutes of longer. These are called panic attacks characterized by a fear of disaster or of losing control even when there is no real danger. A person may also have a strong physical reaction during a panic attack. Panic attacks can occur at any time, and many people with panic disorder worry about and dread the possibility of having another attack.

PARANOID SCHIZOPHRENIA - Paranoid schizophrenia is a mental illness that involves false beliefs of being persecuted or plotted against. It is distinguished by paranoid behavior including delusions and auditory hallucinations. Paranoid behavior is exhibited by feelings of persecution, of being watched, or sometimes, this behavior is associated with a famous or noteworthy person, a celebrity or politician or an entity such as a corporation. Paranoid schizophrenia is a subtype of schizophrenia in which the patient has delusions (false beliefs) that a person or some individuals are plotting against them or members of their family. It is difficult or impossible for others to convince them that they are not the target of a plot. People with paranoid-type schizophrenia may display anger, anxiety, and hostility. The person usually has relatively normal intellectual functioning and expression of affect. Paranoid schizophrenia is a lifelong disease, but with proper treatment, a person with the illness can attain a higher quality of life.

SCHIZOPHRENIA - Schizophrenia is a chronic severe, debilitating mental illness characterized by disordered thought, abnormal behaviors, and anti-social behaviors. It is a psychotic disorder, meaning the person with schizophrenia does not identify with reality at times. There usually are drastic changes in behavior and personality.

SOCIAL PHOBIA - (Also called Social Anxiety Disorder) A strong fear of being judged by others and of being embarrassed. Everyone has felt anxious or embarrassed at one time of another. For example, meeting new people of giving a public speech can make anyone nervous. People with social phobia worry about these and other things for weeks before they happen.

SCLC – (Southern Christian Leadership Conference) An African-American civil rights organization, SCLC, which is closely associated with its first president, Martin Luther King Jr; had a large role in the American civil rights movement.

SWAT Team – (Special Weapons and Tactics) – An elite unit within a police force, used for exceptional situations that require increased firepower or specialized tactics.

STIGMA – A set of negative and often unfair beliefs that a society has about something; A mark of disgrace that sets a person apart. When a person is labelled by their illness they are seen as part of a stereotyped group. Negative attitudes create prejudice which leads to negative actions and discrimination. Stigma brings experiences and feelings of shame blame.

TRAUMA – Single or multiple distressing events that may have long lasting and harmful effects on a person's physical and/or emotional well-being.

WALK-A-MILE IN MY SHOES RALLY – A walk for behavioral health and developmental disability advocates from around Michigan to gather at Michigan State Capitol and educate the public and legislators about mental health.

WOMEN'S SUPPORT GROUP – Women providing mutual support to improve their coping skills. Group Type: Therapeutic/Didactic. The Group is for women only.

Useful Links for Learning About and Living With Depression/Schizophrenia

www.nimh.nih.gov

1-866-615-6464 (toll free) -- The National Institute of Mental Health (NIMH) offers information on mental illnesses and treatment options.

www.caregiver.org

1-800-445-8106 (toll free) -- The Family Caregiver Alliance is a nationwide public voice for caregivers of loved ones with chronic health conditions.

www.healthyminds.org

Healthy Minds is the American Psychiatric Association's online resource for anyone seeking support or facts about mental illnesses.

www.healthyminds.org/More-info-For/African-Americans.aspx

Healthy Minds, the American Psychiatric Association's online resource, provides support and facts on mental illness for African Americans.

www.bazelon.org

1-202-467-5730 – Bazelon Center for Mental Health Law handles general legal
Issues – 1101 15th St. NW, Suite 1212 –Washington, DC 20005

www.nmha.org

1-800-969-6642 – National Mental Health Association – 2001 N. Beauregard St., 12th Floor – Alexandria, VA 22311

www.mhselfhelp.org & www.cdsdirectory.org

1-800-553-4539 – National Mental Health Consumers' Self-Help Clearinghouse offers referral and information services – 1211 Chestnut St., Suite 1207 – Philadelphia, PA 19107

www.ada.gov

1-800-514-0301 – Americans with Disabilities Act handles employment issues – U.S. Department of Justice – Civil Rights Division, Disability Rights Section – 950 Pennsylvania Ave NW – Washington, DC 20530

Depression and Schizophrenia Treatment Links and Resources

www.healthyminds.org/more-info-for/hispanicslatinos.aspx

Healthy Minds, the American Psychiatric Association's online resource, provides support and facts on mental illness for Hispanics/Latinos

www.mentalhealthamerica.net

Mental Health America, formerly the National Mental Health Association, is the country's oldest and largest nonprofit organization for mental health and mental illness.

www.nami.org

1-800-950-NAMI (6264) -- The National Alliance on Mental Illness (NAMI) supports people with mental illness and their families and friends.

www.nami.org/multicultural

1-800-950-NAMI (6264) -- The National Alliance on Mental Illness (NAMI) Multicultural Action Center supports people of diverse backgrounds who are affected by mental illness.

<u>www.janssen.com</u>

This site offers information about treatment options for mental illness provided by Janssen Pharmaceuticals, Inc. You can also call 1-800-JANSSEN.